Francis
in All His Glory

by Burke Wilkinson

NOVELS

Proceed at Will

Run, Mongoose

Last Clear Chance

Published as the trilogy
The Adventures of Geoffrey Mildmay

Night of the Short Knives

BIOGRAPHIES FOR ALL AGES

The Helmet of Navarre

Cardinal in Armor

Young Louis XIV

Francis in All His Glory

NAVY TRUE STORIES

By Sea and by Stealth

ANTHOLOGY

Cry Spy!

FRANCIS
IN ALL HIS
GLORY

BURKE
WILKINSON

Farrar, Straus & Giroux

New York

FOR PATRICIA
with love

Contents

Illustrations

Principal Characters

The Royal Family

Francis I, King of France (Count of Angoulême and Duke of Valois)

Louise of Savoy, his mother, twice Queen Regent of France

Marguerite of Angoulême, his sister

Claude, Queen of France, his wife

The Dauphin Francis, heir to the throne

Henry, Duke of Orléans, younger brother of the Dauphin

The Arch-Rival

Charles V, Holy Roman Emperor and King of Spain

The King and Queen of England

Henry VIII and Catherine of Aragon

The Great Conspirator

Charles de Montpensier, Duke of Bourbon and Constable of France

Two Popes

Leo X

Clement VII

The Soldiers and Courtiers

Charles, Duke of Alençon, husband of Marguerite of Angoulême

Pierre du Terrail, Seigneur de Bayard, the *chevalier sans peur et sans reproche*

Guillaume Gouffier, Seigneur de Bonnivet, Admiral of France

Odet de Foix, Vicomte de Lautrec

Jacques de Chabannes, Marshal de La Palice

Robert de La Marck, Sieur de Fleuranges, known as the "Young Adventurer"

Anne, Duke of Montmorency, Constable of France in his turn

The Former Kings and Queens of France

Charles VIII

Louis XII

Anne of Brittany, wife first to Charles and then to Louis

Mary Tudor, second wife of Louis

The Artist and the Artisan

Leonardo da Vinci

Benvenuto Cellini

The Royal Mistresses

Françoise de Foix, Duchesse de Châteaubriant

Anne de Pisseleu de Heilly, Duchesse d'Étampes

The Ultimate Victim

Jacques de Beaune, Baron of Semblançay

Francis
in All His Glory

Francis I, portrait by Clouet

Prologue

He looked like the Renaissance. With his bold profile and merry, slanting eyes, he seemed to embody all that was sensuous and beautiful in that high-noon time of the world's history. Perhaps he was lucky that both Titian and Clouet painted him, and that the two portraits are in the Louvre today. Superimpose them, and you have a fair idea of what the man was like. The vigor, the mockery, and the elegance still come strongly through.

What, in this less exuberant time, can we learn from the life of Francis, the first of his name to be King of France?

He was brave, and bravery always carries its own message. Yet there were braver men in his own day—Bonnivet and La Palice and the Chevalier Bayard among them. He had taste and something of the common touch—but taste was the currency of Renaissance princes, and it is not so remarkable to have the common touch if you are the monarch.

He was less cynical than many of his contemporaries—certainly he lacked the ultimate cynicism of Caesar Borgia, whom Machiavelli signaled out as the prototype of Renaissance prince. The element of cruelty, which Borgia possessed so coldly and which Machiavelli condoned as part of the necessary equipment of a leader, was almost totally lacking. (He did allow his Minister of Finance, Jacques de Semblançay, to go to the gallows, as we shall see. But, in the main, he was a compassionate man in an age that glittered with cruelty.)

What can we learn? First of all, the fact that he was himself capable of learning. Early in life he went to war the way a medieval knight did. War was the pastime, the noblest profession, and just about the only one for king or paladin. In the early sixteenth century, politics were simply an extension of war by other means, when the money for war-making temporarily gave out. \ *Clausewitz*

The battle of Pavia, where his headlong courage led to disaster, taught him a great deal. The long months as the prisoner of Charles V engraved the lesson in bitter grief.

In a way it was Francis's bad luck to have as arch-rival that first post-Renaissance man. Charles V, frail Hapsburg emperor of the protruding jaw and cold eye, had the shrewdness of a shopkeeper of his own Low Countries, the fierce Spanish pride of his adopted land. He surrounded Francis's territories and seemed at times to overwhelm him. Yet he never quite did so, and Charles's patchwork empire fell apart while France survived to become the first great modern state.

Woman-raised, with Louise of Savoy as ever-adoring mother and Marguerite of Angoulême as ever-enchanted sister, he liked the company of women. So his became a court where women shared in the daily life as never before.

Yet as he grew older there was a streak of melancholy, of incipient boredom despite the wars and threats of war, the endless, almost obsessive hunting, the boisterous Court. See him at Chambord, that white palace he built in the scrub country south of the Loire. The rain is drumming on the windows and it is too wet to hunt. Restless, unhappy with some new infidelity of his own Duchesse d'Étampes, he takes a diamond ring and scratches away on the pane:

> *Souvent femme varie;*
> *Bien fol est qui s'y fie.*

At least that is what legend says he wrote there. A hundred and fifty years later a less vulnerable, less likable man broke the pane to please another royal mistress. This was Louis XIV, in the first flush of his love for Marie Mancini. So we don't know the exact words that Francis scratched on the glass. But the intent is clear enough: *women are fickle; foolish is he who puts his trust in them.* . . .

Gallantry, gentleness, gaiety, but again that taste of his. Not just the taste to bring Leonardo da Vinci to France, and Primaticcio, Cellini, and Il Rosso. That was their wish as well. Francis had the taste to encourage less-known men like Lescot and Goujon, the taste to lead his workmen as he had once led men in battle, the taste to plan, to dream, to buy and buy again.

Amboise, Blois, Fontainebleau and the Louvre (in their purest parts), Azay-le-Rideau, Chenonceaux, Villers-Cotterêts, Saint-Germain-en-Laye—think of the bracelet of bright buildings on which he left his mark! The crowning splendors of the High Renaissance, they are palaces so perfect that they make perfection seem easy.

Toward the end, although he was jaded and ill, the old fighting spirit flared briefly, as we shall also see. But on the whole his life was a royal progress, an upward journey of the mind and spirit. In its course, he went from glory-hunter to the greater glory of civilized man.

Let's see how it all came about.

BOOK I

The Vigil

Humility kept me company,
and patience never abandoned me.

Chapter 1

MY CAESAR,
MY SON

Charles, Count of Angoulême, was an outlying nobleman of the royal house of Valois. His lands, in the sunny vineyards and farmlands of the southwest of France, were as remote from Paris as he himself was distant from the throne. He was, in fact, a third cousin of King Louis XI. Charles lived mostly at Cognac, on the slow-winding Charente River. He loved good talk and good books, and he was not very warlike for those clashing, clanging times.

When he was twenty-nine, he married Louise, a princess of the ducal family of Savoy. To do so was a little inconvenient, for he had a longtime mistress called Jeanne de Polignac, a small daughter by Jeanne, and a pleasant lazy life. But Louis XI of France, the famous Spider King, decreed the marriage, such marriages of state being part of the web that Louis never ceased to weave.

The marriage took place in 1488, when Louise of Savoy was twelve. She brought with her quite a good dowry, some fertile acres in the province of Poitou and the castle of Romorantin in the lake-filled land called the Sologne. Jeanne de Polignac was wise enough to welcome the new bride with open arms, for she was quite aware that she herself was not royal enough to marry a cousin of the King. As for Louise, she was content to bide her time until she had children of her own to buttress her position as consort and chatelaine.

Among the artists and writers at the civilized little Court of Charles of Angoulême was a man called Testard, whose beautiful illuminated manuscripts have come down to us. In several of them there are likenesses of Louise during these early years. She looks very slim and straight, with light brown hair drawn smoothly back. The nose is prominent and well formed; her strong character also shows in the level gray eyes and small, firm mouth.

During her fourteenth year Louise began to worry because she had not yet conceived a child. Characteristically, she took action. The action involved a famous hermit and holy man called St. Francis de Paule, who lived in a cave along the Loire. His prayers were reported to have helped many barren women. Louise journeyed to his rock-hewn hermitage to enlist his help.

St. Francis, who was nearly eighty years old and had seen a lot of women come and go, was impressed by her spirit. He reassured her that the son she wanted would be hers. Then, in privacy and secrecy, he told her more: the son that she would bear would one day be King of France.

Because she was deeply religious, and because she wanted to believe him very much indeed, she accepted his prophecy implicitly—fantastic though it seemed at the time. She had the good sense to keep it to herself. But from that moment her whole life would be shaped toward its fulfillment.

Louise of Savoy

In 1492 Louise gave birth to a daughter. She called her Marguerite, and concealed her disappointment as well as she could. The daughter's name was well chosen, for in French it means pearl and also a kind of daisy that always turns toward the sun. Marguerite would grow up to be one of the most brilliant and beloved women of her time.

In the same year another birth took place, which made the fulfillment of the secret prophecy of St. Francis de Paule seem more unlikely than ever: Charles VIII, who had succeeded his father as King of France, was presented with a son and heir by his young Queen, the famous Anne of Brittany.

Early in 1494 Louise found that she was pregnant again, and her strong spirit soared. (No one in the liberal-minded, sensual little Court seemed very surprised that Jeanne de Polignac was also with child.) All that summer, life at Cognac, and in the grimmer castle upriver at Angoulême where she and Charles sometimes stayed, was pleasant and placid like the smooth-flowing Charente.

Louise was outdoors in the rambling gardens at Cognac when her labor pains began. The delivery took place under a tree in the soft September night. It was a boy, well formed, robust, lusty from his first cry.

Louise's journal has come down to us, some entries written day by day, others added years later. Here is the triumphant entry, half hope and half hindsight, for Louise's great day of days:

Francis, by the Grace of God King of France and my pacific Caesar, took his first sight of the light of day at

Cognac, about ten hours after midday, 1494, the 12th of September.

A little over a year later, the amiable, easygoing Charles of Angoulême was journeying through Poitou in bitter weather. He caught a chill at a place called Châteauneuf-sur-Charente, and soon developed a burning fever. Louise hurried to his bedside. Despite many doctors, many bleedings, and her fierce, devoted care, he died.

The notation in her journal is terse enough: *"On the first day of January in the year 1496 I lost my husband."*

Louise was only nineteen. She would never marry again, never bear another child. Her son would be her life, his high destiny her destiny as well.

Chapter 2

THE BEGINNING
OF THE GOLDEN QUEST

Charles VIII didn't look much like a king. His head was far too big for his rickety little body. He had bulging eyes, a long, twitching nose, and a narrow chest. Partly to prove himself the valiant warrior he so obviously was not cut out to be, and partly because the noblemen of his Court were clamoring for war, he decided to stage a full-scale invasion of the Italian states to the south and east of his domains.

France's own bitter internal wars were over at last, and her frontiers more secure than ever before. With the death of Charles the Bold, Duke of Burgundy, in 1477, most of that great duchy to the east had fallen to France. Fourteen years later, by marrying Anne, Duchess of Brittany—sole heiress to that almost legendary land—Charles VIII secured his western approaches.

The first step was to make sure that such potential enemies as England, Spain, and the Holy Roman Emperor would stay aloof. So Charles bribed them with lands and money to do so.

There was no question but that Italy was the logical place to attack. She was fragmented into six major city-states or principalities, and dozens of smaller ones. The six consisted of the duchies of Milan and Savoy, the city-states of Venice and Florence, the Kingdom of Naples and the Roman holdings of the Pope. They lived in a kind of uneasy equilibrium with each other which allowed the arts and sciences to flourish. But, militarily, the whole of Italy lay like a great golden plum for the plucking.

Charles had a pretext and some slight justification. The former was the fact that, two hundred years before, one of his own ancestors had temporarily conquered Naples for France. The latter was that Ludovico Sforza, whose hold on the duchy of Milan was anything but firm, had rather trustingly asked for his help.

Anne of Brittany—lame, plucky, "very pretty in the face," as the Venetian ambassador reported—was bitterly opposed to the Italian adventure. She wanted Charles to stay with her and their son and heir, the two-year-old Dauphin, to enjoy the peace and plenty that had come to France. But Charles, his big empty head ringing with tunes of glory, brushed her misgivings aside and rode off to join his troops.

On the same September day in 1494 that saw the birth of his country cousin Francis of Angoulême (later of France), Charles and his army were in Asti on the far side of the Alps. Their show of force was overwhelming. The townspeople, who had prudently opened their gates, stood back to enjoy the spectacle.

First came the infantry, some 17,000 of them, archers and crossbowmen, halberdiers and Swiss foot soldiers with their short, brutal-looking spears. Then came the artillery, thirty-seven huge bronze cannon drawn on heavy carriages, along

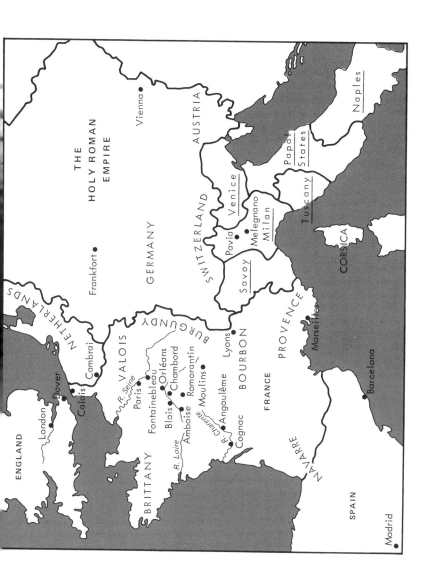

Sixteenth-century Europe

with many culverins and falconets of smaller caliber. Next in the seemingly endless river of men were 7,000 mounted troops, followed by nearly a thousand knights in full armor. Last of all, under a canopy of gold and between two lines of pages in velvet, came the King himself, riding a splendid black horse. His crown, his long blue cloak, and his curved breastplate gave an illusion of dignity and power. But his eyes still bulged, and close-to there was something fatuous about the fixed smile.

All the way down the boot of Italy, the invasion went like clockwork. Now and then a fortress or town put up a token resistance. For the most part, it was Asti all over again. When he reached the borders of the duchy of Milan, Ludovico Sforza almost prostrated himself in his welcome.

In Rome, Charles and Alexander VI, the cynical Borgia Pope, had a long series of talks while the French troops swaggered through the Imperial City. Finally, Alexander gave the King the great Papal blessing, the invading army went swinging on down to Naples, and the Pope heaved a vast sigh of relief.

In Naples, King Ferdinand slipped out the back gate just as Charles was making his usual triumphant entry.

Naples was the high-water mark of the campaign. Now the ebb tide set in.

The kingdoms and principalities which felt alarm over the way the French had rolled through Italy quickly closed ranks. Two of the city-states—Venice and Milan—took the lead, forming the Holy Coalition with the express purpose of driving Charles VIII back over the Alps. Spain, the Holy Roman Emperor Maximilian, and even the nimble Pope

Alexander added their power and prestige. The agreement was signed on March 31, 1495.

Meanwhile, Charles kept writing home that he was about to start the long march north again. But Naples, whose skies were bluer and whose women were fairer than anything he had ever seen, held him in a silken trap.

At last, two months after the Coalition was signed, Charles set out for France, leaving some 8,000 men—almost half his remaining forces—to hold Naples. He placed his cousin Gilbert of Bourbon in command there, a brave man who never got out of bed before noon if he could help it. This proved to be a mistake, as the Neapolitans, now thoroughly aroused, were getting up earlier and earlier to plot and to arm.

The homeward zeal of the French troops was almost as great as the lust with which they had surged south nine months before. Until July, they made good progress. But at Fornovo, in the duchy of Parma south of the Po Valley, Charles found his escape route blocked. The Coalition army of 30,000 men, commanded by the Marquis of Mantua, was deployed there in full battle array.

Foolish as he was, Charles had plenty of spirit, and his speech to his men showed it: "Gentlemen, you will live or die with me, will you not? They are ten times as many as we, but you are ten times better than they."

They were indeed the flower of French chivalry, and at last they had a chance to prove their valor before their King.

There was the hard-bitten Pierre de Rohan, already a Marshal of France, and the more subtle but equally experienced Prince Louis de La Trémoille. Among the younger men who would earn their spurs that day were the Marquis

Anne of Brittany receiving a book on the Italian campaign

de La Palice and the Chevalier Bayard, just turned twenty. Bayard's matchless fame as the *chevalier sans peur et sans reproche*—the knight without fear and above reproach—lay all ahead.

Absent was Louis, Duke of Orléans, next in line for the throne should anything happen to the little Dauphin. Louis had been left in the north of Italy, where he was hard pressed to hold the city of Novara.

The battle was short but furious. The French charged first, withstood the shock of a counter-charge, and charged again. At one point Charles was so far ahead of his body-guard that he was almost completely surrounded by the enemy. He defended himself heroically, until some royal troops saw his plight and spurred to his rescue. The Coalition forces finally withdrew, leaving the field in good order. Wisely, Charles decided not to follow up his victory. Borrowing a cloak, he slept that night in an abandoned farmhouse, well pleased with the day's work.

The next day the French moved north again. On his way north Charles scattered the Milanese forces that were pressing Louis of Orléans at Novara, raising the siege. Then the little army hurried back across the Alps.

When Charles reached Blois, he was given a hero's welcome by Queen Anne. But the next day there was alarming news from Amboise, down the Loire: the three-year-old Dauphin had fallen ill. Three days later he was dead.

Anne of Brittany was so stricken with grief that she never quite recovered, although she would bear many more children.

Charles VIII, saddened, spent his time beautifying Amboise and planning another invasion. He had brought more than a score of Italian architects, sculptors, and artisans with him, including a trainer of parrots, and he put them all to work.

Louis of Orléans, who at thirty-three was six years older than the little King, was able to contain his grief. Heir apparent now, he watched and waited.

Down in Cognac, Louise of Savoy studied her son Francis in his cradle with love and pride. He was not yet a year old, but so strong and healthy that her heart leapt. He already had those narrow, merry brown eyes, and the famous laugh was fast becoming rather more of a chortle than a gurgle.

Watching, she dreamed her dreams. They were far more practical than the mirage-like dreams of little King Charles, whose luck, in any event, was fast running out.

Chapter 3

"THIS FRANCIS WHO IS ALL FRENCH"

Louise and Francis were at Cognac when a courier brought the startling news: Charles VIII was dead. Hurrying to see a tennis match in the grassy moat at Amboise, the little King had hit his big, empty head on the low stone door to the gallery. At first he seemed all right, and watched the players awhile. But soon he went into spasm and shock. Not daring to move him, his courtiers laid him out on a mattress in the gallery and there, nine hours later, he died.

So, on April 7, 1498, "Cousin Louis" of Orléans became King Louis XII of France. Francis, not yet four, was for the moment heir apparent to the throne.

For many years Louis had been married to Jeanne, the saintly, deformed daughter of Louis XI. Since she was childless, Francis's succession seemed only a matter of time. It looked as if St. Francis de Paule's prophecy and Louise of Savoy's dream were nearer reality than even Louise had dared hope.

Louis XII was a much more balanced and sensible man than his predecessor. At thirty-six, he also was a man who had lived hard, fought hard, and been imprisoned for open rebellion against Charles VIII. He was lean and vigorous from many years in the saddle as passionate hunting man as well as bold soldier. He had pleasant, easy manners with everyone, despite the fact that, in his time of rebellion, he had acquired quite a few enemies.

When the throne was his at last, Louis made a much-quoted remark that has both style and a royal ring to it: "The King of France avenges not the wrongs done the Duke of Orléans."

He and Louise of Savoy were good friends. So, shortly after his coronation at Rheims, she hurried to Paris to press Francis's claims. She wanted her son to be named Duke of Orléans in his turn, for this title traditionally went to the male relative nearest to the throne. She wanted him to have all the honors and attendants that went with high rank.

Louis greeted her in his pleasant way but refused her request. He did agree to make Francis Duke of Valois, a newly created title with lesser lands. But it soon developed that he had other plans for the succession.

In brief, Louis had decided to marry again.

Even before Anne of Brittany married Charles VIII, Louis had been in love with her. Now she was a widow, still young, still appealing. Moreover, there was a clause in her marriage agreement with Charles saying that, if anything should happen to the King, she should marry his successor. This was to prevent that great duchy of hers from being lost to France. Now something *had* happened to Charles, and Louis was his crowned and anointed successor. The only flaw was that he had a wife, and a saintly one.

Louis's most influential advisor was a shrewd, capable man

called Georges d'Amboise. He took over so many of the King's responsibilities that Louis's comment, when pressed to take action on some decision or decree, has become part of the language: "Let Georges do it."

In this instance Georges did it very well. He knew that Pope Alexander VI was a man who could be bribed. And he also knew that Caesar Borgia, Alexander's coldly ambitious son, needed a French wife and a French title to give support and substance to his drive for power in Italy.

Amboise persuaded Louis to make Caesar Duke of Valentinois and to give him a French princess, Charlotte d'Albret, for a bride. Alexander in turn annulled Louis XII's marriage. Jeanne retired, weeping, to a convent and Louis promptly married his Anne of Brittany. A cardinal's hat from Pope Alexander was Georges's reward for his part in this deftly cynical deal.

Louis wanted a son and heir as much as he wanted Anne. Late in 1499 Anne bore him a daughter—and Louise of Savoy sighed with relief.

Between 1500 and 1503 Anne miscarried several times, but in 1503 she produced a son. Louise's entry in her journal tells the story: "He could not impede the exaltation of my Caesar, for he did not live."

The idea of Francis's "exaltation" held no great appeal for Louis XII. But the King was a man with a lot of common sense. Whether he himself liked it or not, his heir apparent must be trained for royal responsibilities. He ordered Pierre de Rohan, now Marshal Gié—the tough, ambitious soldier who, along with Georges d'Amboise, was his most trusted advisor—to take over Francis's upbringing. At the same time he instructed Louise of Savoy to bring her son to the Loire valley, where he could be nearer the Court.

Louis himself lived most of the time at Blois. But he was in process of tearing down the old feudal castle there and building himself a beautiful new brick wing. So Louise, her daughter Marguerite, and Francis, now Duke of Valois, moved first to Chinon and then to Amboise, twenty miles down the Loire from Blois.

The sunny, remote period of Francis's early childhood was over. Gié, who was masterful but no master of tact, sparred with Louise at every turn. He fired the head of her household, Jean de Saint-Gelais, of whom she was very fond, and he forbade Francis to sleep in the room of Jeanne de Polignac, who was so attached to the whole family. The implication was that Louise and Saint-Gelais were far too friendly, and that Louise's late husband's mistress was too raffish an influence on four-year-old Francis.

Demure on the surface, straight of back, and level of eye, Louise submitted to these measures, biding her time. When Gié gave Francis a pony, and the pony ran away with him, she poured her feelings into her diary, as she added another reason for hating the Marshal:

> *On the 25th of January, 1501, at about two hours of the afternoon, my King, my lord, my Caesar and my son, near Amboise was carried across the fields by a hackney given to him by Marshal Gié, and the danger was so great that those who were present considered it to be hopeless. But God, protector of widows and defender of orphans, did*

Amboise

Samuel Chamberlain

*not abandon me, knowing that if such ill fortune should
deprive me of my love I should have been too unfortunate.*

In actual fact, Francis was already turning into a fine
horseman. He was big and strong for his years, somewhat
accident-prone as he would be all his life, and, like his sister,
full of good looks and good health.

On the surface, the relationship between Louise and Anne
of Brittany, her neighbor at Blois, was cordial enough. But
they hated each other cordially underneath. Louise envied
the Queen her power and position; Anne envied Louise her
two splendidly healthy children. Her own little daughter
Claude was turning out sickly and somewhat lame, and her
sons were never to be.

By Salic law, which was centuries old, the French crown
always descended in the male line, so Claude could not become queen in her own right. Still, she was a great prize,
for Brittany would some day be hers.

In those days royal children were betrothed almost at
birth. Anne wanted Claude to marry a Hapsburg prince
called Charles of Austria. Louis, who liked peace in the
family, rather tamely agreed. Georges d'Amboise believed
Claude should marry Francis of Valois for many reasons,
above all to keep Brittany a part of France.

The people of France wanted this too, and the news of a
possible Austrian marriage disturbed them deeply. The pressure on Louis grew so great that he took a most unusual

step. He called together the Estates General, representing the three estates—clergy, nobility, and commoners who served the crown—to give them a chance to air their wishes. (Secretly, he was in agreement with the marriage to Francis, but he liked to indulge his wife, and felt sorry for her, too.)

Several hundred strong, the three estates met at Tours on May 10, 1506, and again four days later at nearby Plessis-lez-Tours.

The second meeting was the famous one. It was held in the great hall of the castle. Louis, thin and worn from a recent illness, opened the session from his raised throne. Beside him under the blue-and-gold canopy were Francis of Valois and Cardinal d'Amboise. At twelve, Francis, in an ermine cloak and wearing a splendid sword, looked handsome and almost full-grown, for he was very tall for his age.

Thomas Briçot, the learned canon of Notre-Dame, made the opening speech for all the deputies. He praised Louis's just rule—the appointment of fair-minded judges, the reduction of taxes, the peace and tranquillity of the realm. For such accomplishments as these, Briçot said, Louis would go down in history as the "father of his people."

One contemporary chronicler records in this way the moving scene that followed:

> *At these last words loud cheers rang out; emotion was general and reached the King himself, who shed tears at hearing the title which posterity and history were forever to attach to his name.*

Then Briçot came to the heart of the matter. With all the

deputies kneeling, he entreated the King to give his only daughter in marriage to "my lord François, here present, who is all French."

The King, pretending some astonishment, said he would confer with his counselors and with the princes of the blood, and then give his answer. Five days later, while a frozen-faced Queen Anne listened by his side, Louis agreed to the betrothal. At the same time he gave public recognition to the fact that Francis, his son-in-law-to-be, was truly the heir to the throne.

Then he granted the deputies leave to go.

Here was a great step for "ce François qui est tout français," in Briçot's phrase. As son-in-law and officially recognized Dauphin of France, he had moved to the very foot of the throne.

Chapter 4

HEIR APPARENT, HEIR APPRENTICE

Few boys growing up were ever as adored as Francis was by his mother and sister. But the adoration of Louise differed from the adoration of Marguerite. The mother's love was not unmixed with self-interest and the ability to criticize. She loved her son in part for the power and rank that she would share with him if the crown were ever his. Nor was she unaware that he was becoming bold and reckless and profligate as he grew, and she took measures to discipline his wildness and channel his great energies.

Marguerite's love was less worldly. It was a kind of passionate tenderness, and it lasted all her life—through two unhappy marriages of her own and much sadness. Marguerite was as modest as she was beautiful: her verses about her own role as a member of the celebrated trio show this in a touching way:

> Such boon is mine, to feel the amity
> That God hath putten in our trinity
> Wherein to make a third, I, all unfitted
> To be that number's shadow, am admitted.

If Francis was woman-raised and lapped in love—as he most certainly was—he was anything but soft. At Amboise, he and his chosen comrades fought mock battles, hunted, wrestled, grew skilled with bow and arquebus and lance. They took turns attacking and defending model castles. As time passed, the click of wooden sword on wood in the castle courtyard changed to the clang of steel on steel.

In 1504 Marshal Gié, Francis's ambitious guardian, was disgraced for letting his will-to-power show too nakedly. Louise was delighted when an elegant, gifted Gascon called Artus Gouffier, sieur de Boisy, took his place. (Gouffier's younger brother, Bonnivet, became one of Francis's closest friends and, later, Admiral of France.)

Among the other comrades during those boisterous years at Amboise was Charles de Montpensier, a strong, sullen youth who would one day be the traitorous Duke of Bourbon. Chevalier Bayard rode in from time to time between wars, modest as always but with stories of battle that made his listeners' hearts beat faster—and the *chevalier sans peur et sans reproche* more than ever a hero to be worshipped.

But Francis's closest friend was Robert de La Marck, sieur de Fleuranges. Years later, when a prisoner of war, Fleuranges wrote his memoirs and they form a priceless record. He called himself the "Young Adventurer," and here is an early entry that tells how he came to know Francis:

The Young Adventurer having in his time read some books about bold knights of time past and also having heard tell of many adventurers made up his mind to see the world.

Marguerite of Angoulême

Fleuranges, who was all of nine years old, asked his parents to let him go to the Court of King Louis. Surprisingly, they agreed and sent him off to Blois, well escorted by trusted family retainers.

The memoirs go on to tell how Louis greeted him in his friendly way:

"My son, you are very welcome. You are too young to follow me and so I will send you to M. d'Angoulême, who is your own age."

"Sire, I will go where it pleases you to order me."

. . . and the said sieur d'Angoulême and the Young Adventurer found themselves almost the same age and height, and they soon became good friends.

Fleuranges was born for war, and made for war. He had a straight, strong nose, a stubborn chin, long blond hair, and very clear blue eyes, which shone with a cold and tranquil energy. He would in time become a Marshal of France and a soldier whose prowess was second only to the Chevalier Bayard's. His laconic memoirs form a perfect counterpoint to Louise of Savoy's fiercely subjective journal.

Predictably, the time came when Louis XII summoned Francis to Blois to take his place as heir apparent and son-in-law-to-be. Louise was very upset: "On August 3 [1507] my son went away from Amboise to be a courtier and left me all alone."

Alone . . . alone . . . alone . . . the words echoed down the too quiet corridors of the castle.

Soon Louise and Marguerite headed south for Cognac. While biding her time there, Louise improved her lands and kept her powerful connections in good repair. Fortunately, next to her children, her first thought was for money and the power it brought. This preoccupation would see her through some thin years of waiting.

At Court, Francis throve. Almost six feet now, with a deepening voice and a ringing laugh, he seemed to be everywhere at once—hunting, dancing, studying a little on wet days, already quite aware of the ladies of the Court. He shared Louis XII's passion for the hunt, and they ranged far afield across the mild, open country of Touraine. Louis also shared with Francis what he had learned in the way of statecraft, and some of his friendly, easy way with people rubbed off on the younger man. In a situation that could have been awkward, a warm, two-way affection developed between King and heir apprentice.

There was only one flaw: Louis refused to let Francis go to war. It was not so much that he was precious to the King as that he was invaluable to France.

Louis seemed always to be planning wars, sending his generals off to war, or himself leading men in battle. On the subject of Italy his good domestic common sense deserted him completely. From the moment in 1498 when he was crowned King of France and "King of Naples and Jerusalem and Duke of Milan" as well, he served notice that he would invade again. "Jerusalem" was only lip service to the old medieval spirit of the Crusaders. But Italy was an obsession.

Through a Visconti grandmother he claimed Milan, and through a royal Anjou forebear, Naples.

(After Charles VIII pulled out, Ferdinand II had quickly reconquered Naples, clapping the sleepy Gilbert of Bourbon in prison, where he could doze away all day.)

In all, between 1498 and 1515, Louis staged six invasions. Cynical coalitions with high-sounding names formed and re-formed like pieces of glass in a kaleidoscope—some in support of Louis, some against. In 1509 he led his army to a bloody victory over the Venetians at Agnadello. In 1512 his brilliant nephew, Gaston de Foix, beat "The League of the Holy Union" at Ravenna—the coalition in this instance including the Pope, the Venetians, and Ferdinand of Spain. This hollow victory rang more hollow still when Gaston de Foix lost his life, almost at the exact moment of triumph.

Bayard's exploits in these campaigns added to his growing fame. Sulky Charles de Montpensier carved himself a share of the glory. So did sturdy Bonnivet.

Francis of Angoulême and Valois chafed.

At last, in 1512, when he was eighteen, his chance did come. This is the way Fleuranges remembers what happened:

The King dispatched M. d'Angoulême and sent him into Guyenne as lieutenant general, he having a fine army, and there he fought some fine skirmishes at the foot of those mountains . . . When the Spaniards saw how strong the French were they withdrew, abandoning all, and Saint-Jean-Pied-de-Port was retaken by the French.

Francis was in command at the successful siege of Saint-Jean in the Pyrenees. He also led a diversionary raid toward San Sebastian. But the campaign on the whole was a bitter and useless one.

Next year—1513—the roof fell in on Louis XII and his dreams of conquest. It was in fact one of the bleakest years in French history (and one in which Francis would see sharp action). It seemed as if the whole civilized world was joining forces against the aging, ailing King. The new coalition included the Holy Roman Emperor, Maximilian I, wily Ferdinand V of Spain, and Leo X, the recently crowned Medici Pope, who was both adroit and ambitious. They were joined by Henry VIII of England, just turned twenty-two and anxious to find a winning cause behind which to put his burly strength.

In April, the French forces in Italy lost the battle of Novara to Swiss mercenaries of the new league. Fleuranges, the Young Adventurer, was carried from the field with forty wounds—and lived to fight again. The beaten French army retreated to France with as much dignity as it could muster.

Meanwhile, Henry VIII crossed the Channel with 12,000 men, took Thérouanne and Tournai, and put the French cavalry to rout in the "Battle of the Spurs"—so named because there was more use of spurs than swords on the part of the flying French.

At one point in this campaign, Francis and some friends foolishly shed their armor and went swimming. Surprised by the English, they barely made their getaway. Not much glory here. But Francis was learning. He had been blooded, he had tasted battle, and found he liked the taste.

By winter the coalition—after the manner of sixteenth-century alliances—began to come unstuck, and France breathed again.

Over fifty by now, gout-ridden, disheartened by defeat, good King Louis seemed more like the grandfather of his people than the father. Another son had been born dead, and all his Italian aspirations were dead as well.

Yet France had profited indirectly from the Italian campaigns. It was as if she had been fed intravenously by the Renaissance. Her soldiers brought back strange new fruits like the melon, new vegetables called artichoke and asparagus. From Turin and Milan came secrets for making silk, and from Florence something called a fork that one ate with. Words like *imbroglio, parfum,* and *pommade* went into the language, and *pistole* too, named for the Tuscan town of Pistoia, where small arms were made.

If Louis was old and tired, France was alive, even beginning to prosper. And Francis seemed almost a hero in his exuberant youth. Looking at him as he swashed his buckles around the court, loving him but hating him a little too, Louis remarked to one of his courtiers: "We labor in vain. This big boy is going to spoil everything."

Chapter 5

THE PORCUPINE
AND THE SALAMANDER

Francis and the other young bloods at Court spent a lot of time "burying the king." That is, they played a rather cruel game of *who* would become *what* when Louis XII died and Francis succeeded. Charles de Montpensier, already a marked leader in battle, claimed the age-old honor—and the great symbolic sword—of Constable of France. So did a more recent arrival, Anne de Montmorency. Named for his godmother, Anne of Brittany, Montmorency would turn into one of the finest soldier-servants of the crown. Bonnivet, Fleuranges, and the others each saw himself as *duc et pair de France*—the highest rank of nobility, deriving from the twelve legendary dukes and peers of Charlemagne—or as marshal or high admiral.

Watching all the bold new spirits and the swirling life around him, Louis yearned for simpler days at Blois, where he had been born and had lived before he became king. He went to mass every day, liked to garden, kept comfortable but not lavish quarters in his fine new wing. He loved his Anne of Brittany and humored her highhanded ways. Many thought him too indulgent, but Louis had his own comment on that: "One must surely put up with something from a woman when she loves her honor and her husband."

Perhaps in order to see just how far Francis's recklessness with money would go, Louis was generous with his heir. By now Francis's own household was a princely one: there were no less than fifty-nine superior officers—chamberlains and the like—129 court officers of other grades, six huntsmen, ten secretaries and accountants, a doctor, four violinists, a painter and a sculptor.

One historian has said that Francis "had an almost voluptuous sense of gold flowing about him," and the description is apt enough, even for this early stage of his career.

The Italian influence was everywhere now—in the soft lines of the new wing at Blois and its elegant use of brick and stone, in the endless dancing, in the love of Boccaccio's tales and other *novellae*. Michelangelo, super-god of the Renaissance, was as popular in France as he was in his native land, and it was Louis who first tried to lure Leonardo da Vinci northward.

Louis's emblem was the porcupine, although in actual fact he was not a bristling man and most of his own quills turned inward. Now Francis, more appropriately, picked the salamander for his. The salamander was the small, semi-mythical animal who lived in fire and could put out fire. So Francis's motto, in a scroll under the flame-licked animal, was NUTRISCO ET EXTINGUO ("I live by it and extinguish it").

Today, on the walls of many fair French castles, stone porcupines—and, in much greater number, salamanders—proclaim the passion for building which these two monarchs shared.

More and more, women were beginning to figure in the life of the Court, and love as well as glory-to-come was almost palpable in the soft air of Touraine.

Marguerite of Angoulême, married now by royal decree to the dull Duke of Alençon, dreamed of the swaggering Bonnivet, who made no secret of his own passion for her. In a less fiery way everyone—even Francis—loved Claude of France, his bride-to-be. She was short and dumpy, but her features were surprisingly delicate, and her voice was enchanting.

Then there was a most bewitching girl called Françoise de Foix, on whom Francis's ardent gaze would fall in due course. Married to the ambitious Jean de Laval, Seigneur de Châteaubriant, Françoise was a plump brunette with a milky skin and a queenly manner.

In a sense Francis himself, the center of all the flowing, dancing excitement, was not as handsome as he first appeared to be. Certainly the nose was too long. Seen close-to, there was a little fold of shrewdness at the corners of the narrow eyes. And the faun-like smile had something mocking as well as merry about it. But all the rest was superb— the height, the dash, the born sense of leadership, the growing ease with people.

An incident at Amboise is typical of Francis's bold style in his early manhood. One day, to entertain some of his friends, he released a fully grown wild boar in the courtyard of the castle. Beforehand, he had carefully barricaded the court and rigged some dummy huntsmen on a cord for the boar to savage. The spectators were to watch the sport from an open gallery looking down on the court.

At first, all went as planned. Suddenly the boar lost interest in the dummies. He charged the barricades, knocking one down, and came roaring up the stone staircase to the gallery. Francis moved calmly in front of the terrified onlookers, drawn sword in hand. As the boar charged, he sidestepped the snout and the brutal tusks. Then he drove his point home. The boar fell, neatly skewered at his feet, rolled heavily down the stairs, and died in the courtyard below. The relieved spectators cheered and cheered again.

This story is reinforced by the testimony of a bluff contemporary soldier called the Marshal de Vieilleville. He described Francis as "the handsomest and biggest man of the Court, and having such physical strength that in the jousts and tournaments he unhorsed whoever confronted him, and for this power and his fine seat on a horse the princes, nobles and captains . . . considered him the first man of arms of the kingdom."

If 1513 was a near-fatal year for France, the following year was one of sudden, drastic change. In January 1514, Anne of Brittany died at thirty-eight, bitter and exhausted. She left her sorrowing Louis and two daughters—Claude, now fifteen, and Renée, born in 1510.

"Go make the vault big enough for us both," Louis cried in his anguish. "Before the year is out, I shall be with her and keep her company."

Nine months later he married again.

Francis I, portrait by Titian

The decision to do so was both diplomatic and dynastic. His choice was Henry VIII's sister, Mary Tudor. She was eighteen, a perfect English rose with slightly sharp features —blond, elegant, pleasure-loving. Both Louis and Henry wanted this alliance for reasons of state—Louis to turn an enemy of the year before into a friend; Henry to irritate his Spanish father-in-law Ferdinand, who he felt had failed to do his part against France.

As for Mary herself, she was in love with Charles Brandon, newly created Duke of Suffolk, considered the handsomest man in England. But Mary, who was as good-natured as she was elegant, was perfectly willing to marry Louis XII for the time being, provided Suffolk could ultimately become her husband.

Dynastically, Louis still wanted that son.

So, by the impending marriage, all that Louise of Savoy and Francis had worked for and dreamed about was once again in jeopardy.

But first of all, now that Anne of Brittany was dead, the sensible Louis felt that it was important that the long-planned wedding of his daughter Claude and Francis take place.

"I'm going to be married," Francis said one day out of a clear sky to his friend the Young Adventurer. Four days later—on May 14, 1514—he was, with Fleuranges and a few other boon companions in attendance.

The ceremony was held in the chapel of the castle of Saint-Germain near Paris. Claude was still in full mourning for her mother, and Francis wore a simple black, velvet-bordered robe. The presents were in keeping with the down-to-earth practicality of the union. Francis gave Claude a bed and a quilt, and Claude's contribution was a canopy for the bed and some white damask curtains.

After the wedding mass there was a small dinner. Then Francis went off for his usual afternoon's hunting.

The matter of Louis's remarriage moved to stage center.

Francis, who stood to lose so much by it, had learned to dissemble. "The said seigneur d'Angoulême," observed Fleuranges, "wished it to be known, in order to please the King and the English, that he was very pleased with the said marriage."

By September, plans to welcome Mary Tudor to France were ready. Watching sourly, Louise of Savoy noted the royal departure in her journal: "On the 22nd of September, the King Louis XII, very antique and feeble, rode out from Paris to meet his young wife."

In actual fact, Louis seemed younger and more vigorous than he had in years. He was so gratified that Francis was taking the marriage well that he asked his son-in-law to be the official greeter when the royal party met Mary Tudor at Abbeville in the north.

Mary's own retinue was impressive. Besides her ladies-in-waiting, there were 200 archers and 2,000 cavaliers. Francis, in a gold-and-white surcoat, rode into Abbeville on a richly caparisoned mule, while the King waited impatiently in the countryside nearby.

Mary looked radiant. Also in white and gold, she was mounted on a white horse with a golden harness. It was

Queen Claude

clear from this first meeting that she and Francis matched in more than dress. Her French was limited but amusing, and they chatted and laughed all the way to the rendezvous. Francis, in love with life, already half in love with Mary, knew how to make himself agreeable.

When they arrived, a hundred trumpets and cornets blared in welcome. Louis, doing his best to cut a fine figure, made his horse prance, then kissed Mary from the saddle—no small feat for a man of fifty with chronic gout. Francis smiled his white, dissembler's smile and Charles Brandon, Duke of Suffolk, who was in Mary's glittering train, tried hard to do the same.

So began many weeks of revelry by night and by day. On October 9, there was a formal wedding ceremony. Two days later, Mary Tudor was crowned Queen of France at the great basilica of Saint-Denis near Paris—the only English woman ever to be so. Then came a royal procession back to the city, where all the principal squares were festooned with the English rose, intermingled with the lilies of France.

Still acting as a kind of master of ceremonies for his father-in-law, Francis staged some splendid tournaments before an improvised grandstand in the rue Saint-Antoine. In one series of jousts, six Frenchmen tilted in turn against six of the English visitors. Francis himself broke eighteen lances, scoring eight hits. Fleuranges nailed his man three times out of four. But no one could unhorse the Duke of Suffolk, who was immovable as a turret.

When the English contingent finally went home, Suffolk stayed on, Fleuranges tells us, in the lesser role of "Ambassadeur Ordinaire." The Young Adventurer had his own brand of irony, for he notes that Suffolk took this post "willingly, for the company pleased him."

Mary in fact pleased everyone except perhaps Louise of Savoy. She pleased King Louis very much, even though his whole well-ordered life was altered by her coming. It was obvious that she also pleased her new "son-in-law," as she called Francis. (Claude was by now heavy with child, and watched a little sadly from the sidelines while her husband danced and rode and laughed with Mary.)

Suffolk, too, was never far away from the Queen if he could help it, handsome as ever but less stolid and sullen now than he had seemed at first.

There was one ominous note, as the Venetian ambassador, a veteran observer of the French Court, reported to the Doge: "No one speaks of anything but fetes," he wrote. "Unfortunately, no one thinks of an obstacle which terrifies me. To amuse himself with a wife of eighteen, one of the most beautiful princesses of Europe, this is for the King a notable change, and it is very dangerous in his state of health."

By December, Louis was bedridden, flat on his back most of the time. Mary sang to him, and Francis did his best to cheer him, but Louis was dying and he knew it.

Louise went back to her castle at Romorantin in the Sologne, having sharply warned her son to keep away from the enchanting Mary. There in that land of small, secret lakes and languid streams, she would await the inevitable news.

The mist hung like trailing scarves over the bare trees. Occasionally, Louise heard the honking of geese or the call of duck. But mostly she waited in the winter silence that held the land in thrall.

On the first day of the new year, there was a great storm. The wind came howling in from the west across the flat landscape, and Louise's turreted castle rocked with its might. Early the following morning, the sleepless Louise heard a horseman clatter into the courtyard below and quickly sent a drowsy servant to admit him. The horseman turned out to be a courier who had ridden from Paris through the small hours and the waning storm. He brought the tremendous news: *Louis, the father of his people, was dead.*

Remembering another, sadder day, Louise wrote a terse entry in her journal which concealed the joy that lay beneath:

The first day of January I lost my husband, and the first day of January my son became King of France.

At last!

BOOK II

A Kind of Glory

In the year 1515, King Francis,
seeing peace on all sides and himself young,
rich, and powerful, and man of good heart,
began to prepare his army for his own
expedition into Italy.

FLEURANGES, *the Young Adventurer*

Chapter 6

A TIME OF
TRANSITION

The great surging time in history known as the Renaissance was a plank leading from the Middle Ages into the modern world. It was also, more artificially, a trench, a line of demarcation between the two. The plank was two to three hundred years long and as broad as history itself. The trench zigzagged through time and space.

In France, the vital contributing factor was that first invasion of Italy by Charles VIII, and its aftermath. By the time that Francis began making his own warlike preparations, war in Italy was almost second nature to the French.

In the backwash of these wars, Italian craftsmen, political refugees, and ideas flowed into France. It was the sum of their influence which did so much to turn France into the very model of a late-Renaissance state.

Writing about Charles VIII, one historian said that the idea of invasion "kept flitting like a swallow through the open belfry of his brain." Birdbrain that he was, Charles did mirror, both in his drive south and in his dreams of more conquest to come, the mood of France in the 1490's. And Louis XII—such a good, sensible king in many ways—reflected both the spirit of the times and his own feverish compulsion in those innumerable Italian campaigns of his.

For, during all the years of Francis's boyhood, France was stirring with a new sense of power. The Middle Ages—that time of faith and chivalry and superstition—were almost over. The old, mystical beliefs were fast becoming a matter of outward form. There were so many Saints' Days that there was hardly any time left to go on a journey or fight a war. Numerical symbolism was carried to endless extremes —the twelve months of the year were the twelve apostles, the four seasons were the evangelists, and Christ was the year itself. Even a walnut did not escape a weary symbolism: the sweet kernel was Christ's divine nature, the pulpy outer part was His humanity, and the wooden shell the Cross!

From its start in fourteenth-century Italy, a fresh recognition of man's individuality and his destiny was spreading all over Europe. The children of God were beginning to see themselves as masters of their own fate as well. The pagan glories of ancient Greece and Rome—art, architecture, sculpture, literature, law—were becoming as much a part of their inheritance as the articles of Christian faith.

The medieval idea of the chivalrous knight as a nameless doer of good deeds was being replaced by the new cult of the hero—a man of many parts adding up to a most individual and glorious whole.

It is always tempting to use certain key dates as pegs to hang history on. Certainly the fall of Constantinople in 1453 is one such date. It forced the nations of Western Europe to seek other trade routes to the East, and it caused many classical scholars, with a vast accumulation of lore about Greece and Rome, to flee westward. The discovery of printing (1450) and the discovery of America (1492) are of course the other watershed dates of this time of expansion and enlightenment.

That invasion year of 1494 is often convenienty used to identify the start of the second, European-wide phase of the Renaissance, known as the High Renaissance. Actually, Italian ideas had been drifting northward for many years, carried by pilgrim and wandering friar, by Papal legate, political refugee, and royal messenger.

The threads that form the web of history are in fact so many, the pressures that tighten the fabric so varied, that the closely woven pattern itself is bewilderingly complex. Dates help—and labels help if used warily.

Even the word "Renaissance" is a tricky one. No one really knows when it was first applied. We do know that the "rebirth" of interest in classical Greece and Rome was well underway in fourteenth-century Italy. But the label came long, long after. No Frenchman of the early fifteen hundreds ever crept into bed saying, "Good heavens, the Middle Ages are waning"—or ever leapt out of bed crying, "Now I am a man of the High Renaissance."

In actual fact, the strands of medieval pageantry, chivalry, and superstition lasted many centuries after the Renaissance. And there were bright threads of Renaissance-like talent long before the celebrated rebirth itself exploded.

Locked in her feudal ways, steeped in medieval lore and legend, France was a latecomer to the Renaissance. Many of the other countries of Western Europe responded more rapidly than she to the new ideas that were stirring. The field of world exploration is one good example. The Italians Christopher Columbus and Giovanni Caboto sailed for Spain and England respectively, the latter as John Cabot. Vasco da Gama rounded the Cape of Good Hope for Portugal, and Ferdinand Magellan's expedition circled the globe for Spain. In part, these bold men sought the sugar and spices, the gold and silver and coffee and indigo that Moslem power in the eastern Mediterranean denied them. But they also sailed for that love of adventure, that thirst for the unknown, that marked the new age.

Less seafaring than some, the French had a demonstrated gift for land warfare. And Italy beckoned: Italy was their land of gold and spices, their undiscovered country. As inevitably as the sun draws up water, the French armies were drawn south, and drawn again.

This obsession with Italian conquest—mirage and reality —would last far into the sixteenth century and play a spectacular part in Francis's reign.

Chapter 7

ONCE MORE
THE GOLDEN QUEST

France rejoiced in her young new King, and Francis rejoiced in his new crown. The high point of this mutual near-delirium was the royal entry into Paris after the coronation at Rheims.

The procession was long and blazed with color. There were archers in red and blue, and officers of the crown in the velvet and silk and fur of officialdom. The king's gentlemen were clad in white, and the First Chamberlain (La Trémoille) wore red and gold. The Guard of Honor, with fiery salamanders embroidered on their surcoats, raised a cheer from the dense crowd as they swung past.

But it was Francis whom the Parisians had come to see. He rode last of all, in silver from head to foot, on a horse caparisoned in silver. As his horse pranced and caracoled, he threw handfuls of gold and silver into their midst, and the crowd roared and roared again.

Francis's first acts, in those early months of 1515, showed a mixture of authority and common sense which pleased everyone and surprised some.

He had been dazzled by Mary Tudor—she may well have

been the only woman who ever made him lose his head. But now he managed to keep away from her during the six-week period when, in isolation, she waited to see if she was pregnant by the late King Louis. When it was clear that she was not, Francis packed her off to England. On her way home, with his full endorsement, she married her handsome Suffolk. (When Henry VIII heard the news he yelled and fumed, for he had never intended his sister to marry just for love. But he bowed to the accomplished fact.)

The first appointments were excellent. The new Chancellor of France was a short, heavy man from the Auvergne, in the spiny center of France, called Antoine Duprat. Dour and tough-minded, he had served as President of the Parlement and had also been useful to Louise of Savoy in the crucial matter of the disgracing of Marshal Gié.

Wisely, Francis reappointed Louis XII's Secretary of Finance. He was the shrewd, hard-working Florimond de Robertet, and he too was close to Louise of Savoy.

Honors fell richly to those who had been loyal to Francis in the uncertain years. Artus Gouffier, the amiable Gascon tutor, was created Duc de Boisy. Bonnivet, everyone's favorite in love and war, became Admiral of France. For Louise of Savoy, who had known small country households and near-privation, there were the fertile lands of Anjou and Angoulême, both duchies now. Last of all, in the coronation honors, Francis prudently made that dark cousin of his, Charles of Bourbon of the princely lands and near-royal ambitions, Constable of France.

The reason that several of the key appointments were in-

Bonnivet, portrait-drawing attributed to Clouet

tended to please his mother was soon clear: Francis was going to go to war. In his absence, Louise of Savoy would act as Regent of France.

The actual proclamation, issued at Lyons in July, shows that his words already carried a fine ring of authority:

Since we have just right and title to our duchy of Milan, our heritage, which is usurped and held by our enemy and adversary, Maximilian Sforza, after long deliberation we have assembled a great and powerful army with which and the help of God . . . we will reduce him to obedience. All the princes and nobles of our blood will accompany us in this enterprise. And in consideration of this, we have decided to leave the government of our realm to our well-beloved and dear Lady and Mother, the Duchess of Angoulême and Anjou, in whom we have entire and perfect confidence, who will by her virtue and prudence know how to acquit this trust.

There never had been any question but that war would come. Nor was there any real question where Francis would strike. The spell of Italy still lay over France: Milan beckoned, and perhaps Naples too.

Even before the formal proclamation, rival coalitions were forming, with the characteristic speed and cynicism of the time. Very adroitly, Francis was able to arrange four treaties which gave him a free hand. One was with Henry VIII, who for a solid cash payment agreed not to invade France while her King was away. A second treaty, with young

Archduke Charles of Austria, who would soon inherit both Spain and the lands of the Holy Roman Emperor, guaranteed France's northern and eastern flanks from attack. More actively, the Venetian and Genoese Republics signed on as allies, contributing troops and ships.

Maximilian Sforza, Duke of Milan, did some nimble scrambling of his own. With the support of the aging Emperor Maximilian and the equally aging Ferdinand of Spain, he hired a Swiss army of 20,000 men to guard the Alpine passes, where the French were expected to cross into Italy. Papal troops under the command of Prosper Colonna made themselves available to the duke.

The subtle, cultured Pope Leo himself was a bit of an enigma. Two years before, when he succeeded Julius II, he made a revealing remark to one of his Medici kinsmen. "Enjoy we the Papacy," he said, "since God has given it us."

Now his only wish seemed to be to back the winner. He fondly hoped that it would be Sforza, but he was careful to make no personal break with Francis.

The French King had indeed assembled the "great and powerful army" of his proclamation. There were 10,000 French noblemen and knights-at-arms and 30,000 foot soldiers (*fantassins*). These were reinforced by some 10,000 Basque and Gascon volunteers, and 26,000 German men-at-arms (*Landsknechts*) supplied by the friendly Dukes of Lorraine, Gueldre, and Sedan. The artillery included twelve giant bombards weighing three tons each, as well as many long culverins of smaller caliber, and several hundred of the graceful little *faucons,* which fired stone or iron balls the size of oranges.

The nobles and princes were present in good numbers. There was Charles, the morose Duke of Alençon, whose command was the rear guard, and that other, bolder Charles —Montpensier, now Duke of Bourbon and Constable of France—who led the advance. There were three marshals of France—Jean-Jacques Trivulzio and Don Pedro Navarro, soldiers of fortune both, and the newly elevated Jacques de Chabannes, Seigneur de La Palice. There were of course those boon companions of Francis's—Bonnivet, Lautrec, Montmorency, and Fleuranges. There was Louis de La Trémoille, Prince de Talmont, already skilled in diplomacy and war, and Jacques Galiot de Genouillac, the Grand Master of Artillery. And, as always when lives were in hazard and glory the prize, there was Pierre du Terrail, Seigneur de Bayard, the knight without fear and above reproach.

Such were some of the lords and gentlemen-at-arms who went down into Italy with Francis in those fateful August days.

Not wishing to upset Queen Claude, whose child was almost due, Francis slipped away from Amboise in the small hours. Louise of Savoy rode with him as far as Romorantin, rehearsing her plans and duties as regent as they went. Then Francis galloped eastward to join his army.

Meanwhile, Jean-Jacques Trivulzio, grizzled veteran of seventeen battles, had picked up some exciting news. A peasant told him that there was a tiny unknown pass over the Alps, high up in the desolate eastern frontier of France, mostly used by hunters. In some places it was not much more than a narrow ledge, with sheer rock above and below.

Trivulzio inspected the pass and reckoned that it just might do. One reason that he urged its use was that the Swiss were well entrenched in the traditional pass called Susa and could only be dislodged at great cost. Both the Swiss and the Italians held the French in contempt. With fond memories of Novara and the Battle of the Spurs, they thought of them as nothing more than "hares in armor." Down in the Italian plain, Prosper Colonna—hearing a rumor that the Chevalier Bayard was already across the Alps—boasted that he would catch him like a pigeon in a cage.

When Francis made camp, Trivulzio outlined his plan of action. Charles of Bourbon, who had also explored the defile, endorsed its use strongly. Then Francis made the decision, and it was in keeping with his own bold spirit: *Yes, let us try the secret pass.*

It was good luck that Pedro Navarro was one of the first great army engineers. He and his "pioneers"—2,500 of them —set to work building bridges across the snow-fed streams that came boiling down the mountainsides. They cleared out the boulders blocking the trail and filled in the holes. They rigged pulleys to drag the guns, and slings to swing them across the gaping chasms.

Everyone was on foot, with the cavalrymen leading their horses. Their only drink was water, the sole food was bread and cheese. For there were no villages to buy supplies in, no room to carry more. All they saw were the dark pines and the giant peaks, and for the most part all they heard was the roar of the swollen streams.

Every now and then someone would make a false step. A strangled cry . . . a nightmare whinny . . . and a man or horse would go spinning down into the abyss.

The defile itself—the slit between the peaks—was 6,500 feet above sea level. First Bourbon, then Francis with the main body of troops, then Alençon struggled over it and started the descent. Down was worse than up, for the view into the void was far more terrifying. The path itself, creased by ravines, laced by torrents, was as treacherous as ever.

But they made it. In five days the French army did what only Hannibal had ever done before then. Francis, in full armor except for his helmet, was everywhere—encouraging, cursing, laughing, lending his great strength here to swing a cannon, there to restrain a horse in panic. Afterwards, he wrote his mother exultantly:

Nobody who has not seen it would believe it possible to bring horsemen and heavy artillery as we have done. Believe me, madam, it was not without great trouble, and had I not been there our artillery could not have done it.

His pride was pardonable, for it was his triumph in good degree.

Prosper Colonna with some 2,000 horsemen was camped near the headwaters of the Po. He himself was dining in the little walled town of Villafranca. It was a lazy August afternoon, and, despite the warnings that the French were near, he didn't have a care in the world. Within four miles was the formidable fortress of Pinerolo, held by 4,000 Swiss comrades-in-arms. He would march there at his leisure as soon as he had dined.

Marshal La Palice and the Chevalier Bayard had other ideas. They were among the first to ride down into the Piedmont plain, with some 400 men-at-arms. When they reached the swift-running river Po, they were informed by a spy where Colonna was dining.

"We must wake up his wits a little," Bayard said to La Palice. "This moment, let us get into the saddle, with all our troops, that he be not warned by any."

They crossed the river at a secret ford without losing a man.

Bayard was the first to reach Colonna's headquarters, where some archers stood guard. "Yield and utter no sound," he said in a low voice, "else you are dead men."

Some of the guards defended themselves; others fled to warn Colonna.

"Lads," said he, "keep this door a little, till we get some armor to defend ourselves."

But Bayard and his men scaled the windows while the door was being held. Bayard leaped down into the room, crying, "France, France! Surrender!"

Pectore dum firmo pugnam . . . . . suſtentat In hostem
Converso ʃoluit ʃaucius ore mori.

Cum privil.

Le chevalier Bayard

Colonna saw that he was outnumbered and gave up his sword.

Bayard tried to console him. "My lord Prosper," he said, "the fortune of war! Lose one time, win another."

"Would to God . . ." said Prosper bitterly. Then, remembering his Roman manners, "France is a country I have always wanted to see."

Along with the celebrated Colonna, La Palice and the Chevalier Bayard captured several other noblemen to hold for high ransom. They were also richer by a chestful of ducats and many vessels of gold and silver.

It was a fine start for the golden quest.

As the main body of the French army came pouring down into the plain, outflanking the pass at Susa, the Swiss retreated toward Milan, trailing their pikes and dragging their heavy guns behind them.

Chapter 8

QUINZE QUINZE

By early September, the Swiss were in Milan, with the French snapping at their heels. Behind the high, burnt-umber walls of the old city there was great activity. Francis's spies reported that the Swiss could not make up their minds whether to come out and fight or not. The speed of the French descent into Italy, and the spectacular capture of Colonna, had left them in a kind of shock.

September 12 was Francis's twenty-first birthday. With his narrow, mocking eyes, high coloring, and scanty beard he looked very young. But his actions were beginning to show a remarkable maturity. He had entered into negotiations with the enemy on a surprising subject: the possibility of *not* fighting at all. Even though his troops were honed for battle, and the prospect of combat made his own hot blood race, he offered the enemy 600,000 golden ducats and a very favorable peace treaty if they would withdraw to their cantons in the north. His justification for this offer has a modern sound to it, a sweet reasonableness that does him credit: "I would not purchase with the blood of my subjects, or even with that of my enemies, what I can pay for with money."

At first, the Swiss seemed inclined to agree. Scraping together a first payment of 150,000 ducats as bait, Francis sent Lautrec to work out final terms.

In the meantime, he maintained his army on full alert. The main body of the troops were camped at Melegnano, a few miles southeast of Milan on the Lombard plain. But, from a discreet distance, his scouts kept a sharp eye on the gates of the city itself.

They reported that reinforcements from the north were pouring in—Swiss mercenaries whom the beleaguered Maximilian Sforza had been screaming for. By mid-September, 40,000 Swiss were in Milan. Still, Francis's informers within the city said, there was disagreement among their leaders about what to do next. And Francis himself, not wishing to start a long, costly siege, still hoped that a treaty could be worked out.

On the afternoon of September 13, Fleuranges was taking his turn watching the city, which seemed to be drowsing in the early-autumn sunlight. Suddenly, he noted increased activity around the main gate. The sun, beginning to slant now, glinted on breastplate and sword hilt, bronze gun and helmet in growing number as troops came pouring into the countryside. The muffled beating of drums hung in the soft air.

With his trained eye, the Young Adventurer noted that the mountain men looked formidable indeed. The foot soldiers were armed with long, brutal pikes almost triple their own height—longer than he remembered in previous campaigns. Some carried great two-handed swords. There was artillery, too, and small detachments of cavalry were beginning to drift through the olive groves outside the city walls.

Fleuranges put spurs to his horse, wheeled, and galloped away to warn his master.

He found the King in his tent, trying on a new suit of armor. Francis greeted him pleasantly. "You are armed? But we expect peace today."

"Sire," Fleuranges burst out, "we need fool ourselves no longer about peace." He told what he had seen, concluding with his own comment: "Today you'll have battle or I don't know the nation you are dealing with."

Other reports began to come in, confirming Fleuranges's observations. By the thousands now, the Swiss were on the march toward Melegnano. Their leaders had lashed them into fury with promises of booty and reminders that the French were, as always, hares in armor. Another compelling reason to attack was that the Swiss knew that Francis's Venetian allies were coming from the east in forced marches to link up with him and reinforce.

Quickly arming, Francis leaped on his horse and rode to his own front lines. Their location had been well chosen— some high, dry ground in the swampy rice fields of the enormous plain.

Crisscrossed by canals, with occasional vineyards and lines of mulberry trees to break the monotony, the plain itself was not a terrain that lent itself to ambush or subtle maneuver. Even flanking operations were difficult, for the cavalry had to keep to the few roads and pathways across the rice fields.

Harsh shock-charges, close work with sword and dagger, the deadly play of well-placed, well-protected artillery—such would be the order of the day.

The Swiss came steadily on, in three great columns of almost 10,000 men each. They waded the canals, trampled the vineyards, surged through the swamps as if driven by some malevolent fury. As they neared the higher ground where Bourbon's men were lightly entrenched, they closed ranks. A hundred abreast, pikes interlacing, screaming their wild mountain battle cries, they lunged forward. A billowing cloud of dust hid them as they came and blotted out the sun, so that the French artillery had trouble finding their targets.

The Swiss crunched through Bourbon's outposts and had almost reached their main objective, the French guns themselves, when Francis, at the head of 200 horsemen, launched a furious charge into their flank. This slowed the Swiss forward motion just long enough for Galiot de Genouillac's bombards and culverins to score. In the face of a hailstorm of iron and lead which cut down whole ranks at a time, the Swiss recoiled . . . charged again . . . then were driven back across a canal by another counter-charge.

So it went from three to eleven. Above the din and behind the dust, the sun went down. The moon rose and the mortal combat continued. In all, the French made thirty charges, many led by Francis himself. At one point he was forced back on his own artillery so sharply that he dismounted, grabbed a pike, and fought like any foot soldier.

Just after eleven the fitful moon went behind clouds for good, and the two exhausted armies broke off the action by tacit agreement. But it was a wild, tense night, with both sides fearful of surprise attack. Francis stayed "all night a-horseback like the rest" except for a short spell when he stretched out on a gun carriage.

The visor of his plumed helmet was open to the night sky where a pike thrust had pierced it. His blue-steel armor with its golden lilies was dented in a dozen places, and he ached in every joint. But he was fiercely happy just the same. Hadn't his men shown that they could absorb the full fury of the Swiss? Weren't the Venetian reinforcements very near now, and prospects for the next day good?

For a while, lying across the gun carriage, he slept. Then, lance in hand, he mounted his horse again to watch out the night.

Toward morning, Francis straightened the French line, linking up center and wings to form one continuous defense. He also placed his artillery in a new, slightly higher position for more sweeping range.

The Swiss attacked at dawn. Their formations were again the three close-locked columns like battering rams. The central one drove straight for the French artillery, seeking with a desperate valor to overrun and silence the murderous guns.

The French line held magnificently. Finding the range at once, the artillery blunted the charge like an iron fist.

Soon the fighting was furious and widespread.

Bourbon's right flank counter-attacked, and Francis's center held like a rock. Stopped dead there, the Swiss tried a flanking attack against Alençon's left wing and managed to dent it. Some of the French noblemen fled toward the baggage train to the rear, and there were cries that all was lost.

It was the confused, critical moment, with the dust and roar of battle adding to the confusion.

Three things happened almost simultaneously. Bartolomeo Alviano and 300 of his Venetian light horse rode onto the field and went straight into action—fresh warriors to tilt the delicately balanced scales of battle. Alençon's flank dug in its heels and held at last. And Francis unleashed a jolting, thundering charge in which most of his boon companions of the royal household joined him—Bourbon (who seemed to be everywhere that day), La Palice, Bayard, and the rest.

It was too much. In good order, the grim-faced Swiss gave ground. By noon they were in full retreat, with Bonnivet in close and rude attendance. As they neared Milan, the orderly withdrawal became a rout. Many soldiers threw their pikes away as they streamed across the plain. None breathed easily until the city gates had closed at last.

They left twelve thousand of their comrades on the field of battle to attest that the enemy whom they had scorned were no longer hares in armor, or rabbits for scampering.

A kind of exaltation seized Francis, drunk with the strong wine of victory. He let out a shout of joy when he and Bayard met on the still-reeking battlefield.

"Bayard, my friend," he said. "I wish today to be knighted by your hand, for you are known to be the most worthy knight."

Bayard found this somewhat absurd. "Sire, he who is crowned and anointed with oil from heaven . . . and is king of a realm and first son of the Church . . . is knight above all knights."

"Bayard, get on with it! Do as you are told if you wish to be my friend."

Bareheaded, Francis knelt to the chevalier, who struck him lightly on the shoulder—once, twice, thrice.

"The first king I ever knighted," said the modest chevalier.

Then he too was seized with exaltation. He raised his sword and spoke to it. "You are blessed this day to have given knighthood to so fine a prince!" His strong voice rose. "Yes, my good sword, you shall be treasured as a relic and never drawn except against Turk, Saracen, or Moor."

Pointing his sword to heaven, he jumped twice into the air and then clashed the blade back into its scabbard.

Just then Fleuranges, who had been chasing Swiss, rode back onto the field.

"How is this, my friend," Francis called to him. "They told me you were dead."

"Not dead, Sire, and I won't die so long as I can serve you."

"I have just been knighted," said Francis, "and now I pray you to accept knighthood at my hand."

The battle of Melegnano, which the French call Marignan, was one of the glorious moments of French history. Every French schoolboy still knows the date of 1515—"*Quinze Quinze*"—the way we learn *1492* and *1776*. It marked the high moment of Francis's warrior years. It was the first modern battle, in which skillful use of artillery and maneuver narrowly won out over the old concept of an irresistible phalanx of pikemen with little support by gunfire.

Despite French losses, which were about 6,000, or half the number of Swiss dead, the mood of exaltation grew and spread. Old Marshal Trivulzio said that all other battles he had fought paled before it. Writing that night to his mother, Francis went even further: "There has not been so fierce and cruel a battle in the last 2,000 years."

He had high praise for Galiot de Genouillac: "Never did any man use his artillery better"; and for his comrades-in-arms, who "did not spare themselves any more than wild boars at bay."

Louise the Queen Regent and Claude the Queen (whose first child, another Louise, had been born in late August) made a pilgrimage of thanksgiving to a shrine near Blois. There they thanked God for the safety of their "glorious and triumphant Caesar."

Then Louise the Regent ordered that all the castles and towns of the Loire be illuminated to celebrate the mighty victory.

Chapter 9

NEW LINES OF BATTLE FORMING

In those waning hours of the victory, Fleuranges and Bonnivet hounded the Swiss all the way back to Milan. But no final assault was ordered, and later the Swiss mercenaries were allowed to withdraw to their own country unmolested.

These were Francis's own decisions. In making them, he showed considerable wisdom and restraint. The fact was that he could see the time when he would need the Swiss as allies and hired soldiers. A brutal onslaught or near-massacre would have left scars of wounded pride that would not have healed for years.

As it was, the French and the Swiss in due course signed the Treaty of Fribourg, which guaranteed perpetual peace and friendship between the two nations. It remains one of the most unusual treaties in history, for it has never been broken to this day. Soon after Melegnano, Swiss mercenaries were fighting loyally and well in the service of the French King.

This lenient attitude of Francis's was most unusual in a century in which cruelty was condoned and even admired.

Certainly it was considered one of the necessary attributes of a leader.

No one reflected this view more accurately, or stated it with more cool precision, than Niccolò Machiavelli in *The Prince*. Written in 1512, when he was in temporary exile from his duties as a Florentine diplomat, his famous book was not actually published until twenty years later. It was an overnight sensation. "A prince," Machiavelli wrote, "must not mind incurring the charge of cruelty for the purpose of keeping his subjects united and faithful . . . He will be more merciful than those who, from excess of tenderness, allow disorders to arise, whence spring bloodshed and rapine; for those as a rule injure the whole community, while the executions carried out by the prince injure only individuals . . . It is much safer to be feared than loved, if one of the two has to be wanting."

This theme runs all through Machiavelli's book. The model for his ideal prince was Caesar Borgia, that spectacular son of Pope Alexander VI. He tells how Borgia, having gained possession of the Romagna, installed a harsh and able deputy called Remirro de Orca, to bring law and order to those turbulent Roman lands.

De Orca did so at speed but incurred the hatred of the people in the process. "Borgia resolved to show that if any cruelty had taken place, it was not by his orders but through the harsh disposition of his minister. Having found the opportunity, Borgia had him cut in half and placed one morning in the public square at Cesena with a piece of wood and a blood-stained knife at his side. The ferocity of this spectacle caused the people both satisfaction and amazement."

This gruesome measure seemed quite admirable to Machiavelli. The catch was that Caesar Borgia, his prototype prince, died discredited and almost alone, all his ambition and ability turned to dust. Machiavelli ascribed his failure to illness and bad luck, and most of Borgia's contemporaries seem to have agreed.

By contrast, Francis was far ahead of his cynical century. Although he loved the clang of battle and danger's bright face, he almost never killed coldly or cruelly. To his contemporaries his knightly prowess and his chivalry may have seemed a little old-fashioned, but the fact remains that his triumph over the supposedly invincible Swiss made him the most famous prince in Europe.

The victory itself did not please everyone. Henry VIII was furiously jealous. Those two aging monarchs, the German Maximilian and the Spanish Ferdinand, were seriously alarmed.

Hiding his disappointment that the wrong man had won, Pope Leo opened negotiations with Francis at once. The agile Pope proposed a meeting at Bologna, well north of Rome. Quite logically, he feared that if Francis and his army came to Rome they would surge down to Naples. For the great duchy of Milan to be in French hands was alarming, but to have the Kingdom of Naples fall as well would tip the scales of power too heavily.

Francis and Leo met at Bologna in some secrecy. They talked for four days. Then Francis, who had brought Antoine Duprat along to be his chief negotiator, turned matters over to his shrewd, plump little Chancellor. The King kissed the Pope's feet, received absolution, and headed north again, leaving Duprat to hammer out the terms of an agreement.

So, easily enough, Francis was diverted from his plans for further conquest. He had been away for half a year. He was anxious to see his wife and new daughter, his mother and his starry-eyed sister, and to drink the strong wine of victory in his pleasant land of Touraine.

Duprat did well. The agreement or Concordat of Bologna, signed in 1516, confirmed and strengthened the French king in his role as the eldest son of Mother Church. It superseded a treaty, made eighty years before, known as the Pragmatic Sanction of Bourges. The Sanction contained two vital principles. One was the principle that a General Council of the Church had authority over the Pope. A second major clause gave the French king the power to award the high churchly offices in his own land.

Succeeding Popes had found this granting of supreme authority to a Council galling in the extreme. Were they not Vicars of God himself? They were also taking a more and more active part in the creation of bishops and other high officials of the Church all over Europe. Now Duprat drove a shrewd bargain. The French agreed to annul the part about the superiority of Councils, and the Papal negotiators conceded that the French king should continue to make his own ecclesiastical appointments without deferring to the wishes of Rome.

This right of appointments brought a great deal of revenue to the French crown. As a result, both sides were happy with the new treaty. The relationship between the Pope and

Francis became closer than ever—special and without any deep grievance. A few years later, when the Reformation rolled over Europe, France was relatively immune.

On January 13, 1516, Louise of Savoy was reunited with her hero-son. They met at the fortress town of Sisteron in Provence, and her diary records her joy:

> *God knows that I, poor mother, was thankful to see my son safe and sound after all he had suffered and endured to serve the common good.*

Louise herself sparkled. As Regent she had tasted real power at last, and found the taste sweet. The long nose seemed less sharp now, the firm chin looked rounder and somehow gentler. At forty, as well as being a most capable and determined woman, she was almost a pretty one.

The return of the royal party to the Loire was leisurely and triumphant. At Marseilles there were festivities around the clock and a battle of oranges in which Francis took a boisterous part.

At Tarascon, on the lower Rhône, there was news that cast a long shadow: Ferdinand of Spain was dead. His heir was his grandson, Archduke Charles of Austria, sixteen-year-old son of Ferdinand's daughter Joanna the Mad.

Ferdinand left Charles Spain, Flanders, and the untold riches of the New World.

The reason why the shadow over France was long and would grow longer still was this: Charles was also the grandson and heir of the Emperor Maximilian. When he inherited Maximilian's German and Austrian lands as well, France would be surrounded by Hapsburg power—north and east and south. She would be in terrible danger of being crushed to death.

On the surface, the triumphal royal progress rolled smoothly along—up the swift Rhône to Lyons and then west to Touraine. By early summer, Francis was back at Amboise and more than ever in the mood for pleasure. While this mood lasted, Louise of Savoy continued as Regent in all but title. She stayed on at Lyons, which was the nerve center of France as well as its second city. From there she watched as Henry VIII tried vainly to form coalitions against the French, and Leo X tried, more subtly, to be all things to all European contenders.

In the spring of 1516 Maximilian, perhaps sensing that his own end was not far off, made a feeble attempt to conquer Milan. But Charles of Bourbon, whom Francis had left to administer and defend the duchy, faced him down with his scowl and his crack troops. After firing a few cannonades, Maximilian scampered back over the Alps.

Even before Maximilian died, Louise began to line up votes and support for Francis among the German princes who would choose the next Holy Roman Emperor. The title was a fairly empty honor, with no lands attached, but if Charles of Austria won it, along with his Spanish inheritance and Maximilian's German holdings, France would be more vulnerable, more isolated than ever.

The afterglow of Melegnano lasted several years. Francis, less concerned now than he had been in Italy with the "common good," hunted every good day, acquired his first official mistress, planned new pleasure domes along the shallow, sun-flecked Loire.

He had brought Leonardo da Vinci back with him from Italy and installed him in a pleasant little castle near Amboise called Le Clos-Lucé. The pair, the dazzling monarch and the most gifted artist-architect-philosopher-inventor of his age, seemed never to run out of things to talk about. Francis was a good listener as well as a facile talker. Leonardo, in his sixties now and not well, enjoyed sharing his far-ranging views with so agreeable and attentive a king.

The first official mistress was the white-skinned, queenly Françoise de Foix, with whom Francis now fell wildly in love. Everyone around her profited by her elevation to this soon-to-be traditional honor at the French Court. Her brother Lautrec quickly replaced the moody Duke of Bourbon as lieutenant general in Milan. Her husband, Jean de Laval, concealing behind an amiable manner any resentment he may have felt, was in due course made Duc de Châteaubriant.

Meanwhile, gentle Queen Claude, somewhat in the shadow now, produced another daughter in the fall of 1516 and, two years later, the longed-for Dauphin. He was named Francis as the whole nation rejoiced.

Maximilian's death had been so long foreseen that when it actually took place in January of 1519 it was almost an anti-climax. Young Charles of Austria now became the most powerful ruler in the world. Automatically, he also began his great, lifelong rivalry with Francis.

The first clash came in the selection of the new Holy Roman Emperor.

With his jutting jaw that seemed almost a deformity, his glutton's appetite for both food and work, and his small, frail body, Charles did not seem too formidable a rival. But it had been Maximilian's dying wish that he be chosen and this carried a good deal of weight with the seven Electors —the King of Bohemia, the Count Palatine of the Rhine, the Duke of Saxony, the Margrave of Brandenburg, and the Archbishops of Mainz, Cologne, and Trèves.

Louise and Francis sent Bonnivet to Germany to bribe and threaten the seven. The Electors cheerfully accepted huge sums from both candidates. But Charles, who declared that the title was "the thing in the world which he desired most and had most at heart," held back some of his gold, to be paid on delivery of the Imperial crown.

The Electors met at Frankfort on June 28, 1519. They rode, in a great splendor of ermine cloak and ermine-and-gold crown, through the crowded streets of the city. All day, inside the chapel of the Church of Saint Bartholomew, they deliberated, and that night their choice was announced. Predictably, by a good margin in the voting, Charles of Austria was the new Holy Roman Emperor. The German princes had preferred a Hapsburg to a Valois—one of their own race to the flamboyant French warrior-king.

Charles took the title of Charles V. Solemn and studious though he was, he did have a trickle of humor. "My cousin Francis and I are in perfect accord," he said. "He wants Milan and so do I."

Even more character-revealing was his well-known comment about the various languages he had had to learn. "Italian," he said, "is the language of love, French of diplomacy. German is for soldiers and cattle, English for talking to birds."

"And Spanish?" one of his courtiers asked.

"Spanish," said the Emperor, "is for addressing princes . . . and God."

Flemish-born and raised, Charles would in due course become more Spanish than the Spaniards themselves—prouder, more princely, and in even closer communion with the Lord.

Now both he and Francis hungrily eyed Naples as well as Milan, which for the moment Francis possessed. They also began jockeying for Pope Leo's quicksilver friendship. And each in his way sought the support of Henry VIII, whose ambition to play the linchpin role in Europe was as boundless as ever.

Fully alerted now to new dangers, Francis saw clearly what his first move would have to be. He and his "Cousin Henry" (all kings were cousins in those days, by virtue of their kingship) must meet, and they must meet under circumstances which would impress the English monarch with the might and glory of France.

After much diplomatic fencing, time and place were agreed on at last: the countryside of Normandy near Calais in the month of June of the year 1520.

It was one of the most celebrated confrontations of all time. History calls it the Field of the Cloth of Gold.

Chapter 10

THE FIELD OF
THE CLOTH OF GOLD

Francis really did need Henry VIII. England's population of something over three million people was about a fifth of the French sixteen million. But, added together, their combined numbers came close to matching the manpower of Charles V's far-flung lands.

Charles also needed Henry. His two-headed empire, with its single, strong Hapsburg heart, was a conglomerate of duchies, principalities, provinces, and colonies, with not too much in common. All that the thrifty Flemish burghers and the stolid Lowland Dutch shared with the arrogant and adventurous Spaniards was their mutual monarch. Sicily and Luxembourg and the mysterious new world of Hispaniola were other jagged pieces in this Imperial puzzle, not yet put together in any clear pattern.

To Charles, all this was an inheritance rather than an empire. But it was his. A sharp sense of duty and fierce family pride made him determined to fit all the pieces into one workmanlike and working whole.

Behind that long, pale face of his there was the equipment to do so, for he had the tenacity of a bulldog and the disciplined logic of a computer. ("A mind as cold and formidable as an iceberg," one historian said.)

France was his biggest stumbling block, for it lay athwart many of his lands. He could not truly function unless she were humbled and made powerless. Just as France was in grave peril from the Emperor on her northern, eastern, and southern frontiers, so Charles saw France, with her interior lines of communication, as a mortal menace.

So it came to be that Henry of England, instead of being odd man out, found himself courted and cultivated by the two most powerful rulers in the world.

That furious jealousy of his after Melegnano was understandable enough. Although he was older by some three years, Henry had done nothing yet to match Francis either in military prowess or in knightly valor.

He was obsessed with curiosity about his handsome cousin-neighbor.

"What's he like?" he once bawled at the Venetian ambassador, who knew everyone. "Is he taller than I? Are his legs any better than mine?" For all his hearty roast-beef-of-old-England look, Henry was easily moved to rage and tears, and could scream like a fishwife.

Now at last the twain would meet.

Francis as usual was short of money, but somehow he convinced his noblemen that the honor of France was at stake and that their pomp must match the circumstances. Courtiers sold so much of their substance for clothes and armor and horses and livery that one contemporary chronicler

Henry VIII of England, portrait by Holbein

noted that "many bore thither their mills, their forests, and their meadows on their backs."

The meeting place itself was a broad, green field near the town of Guines, which was still held by the English. Thousands of tents were put up—Francis himself directing that the French tents were to be of cloth of gold, with golden apples to crown them.

His own tent was close to the French town of Ardres. It was an immense dome-like expanse of canvas held up by a tremendous pole and an elaborate system of pegs and cords. Unfortunately, a wind of gale force just before the meeting tore up the pegs and snapped the cords, so that the tent lay like a collapsed balloon. Francis took residence in the old castle of Ardres.

The English, who were meant to be dazzled, actually outdid the French in the magnificence of their display. Henry's quarters were a prefabricated palace of wood and glass, 128 feet square, made in England by 1,100 skilled workmen, brought over by sea in sections, and quickly set up. With its fountains that spurted wine, its tapestried great hall and canvas-hung façade painted to look like stone, it was the wonder of wonders.

Opposite his wooden palace, Henry set up a huge statue of a savage with his own not-very-subtle inscription on it: "He whom I back wins."

Just before Henry sailed from Dover for the tremendous encounter, something happened which gave him a wonderful, lifting sense of his own power: Charles V, Holy Roman

Emperor (though not yet crowned), made an urgent visit to England to meet and woo him.

Charles was Henry's nephew by marriage, for his mother's sister was Catherine of Aragon, Henry's first queen among many. When Charles heard of the planned meeting between his uncle-by-marriage and Francis of France, he acted with a speed and skill which showed that he was already the master of his own great destiny. Although a dangerous revolt was flaring among his new Spanish subjects, he took ship for England in a matter of days, and arrived in late May of 1520.

The timing was perfect. Charles's behavior was so deferential that Henry was flattered and impressed. The English King found that he very much enjoyed playing fond uncle and wise counselor to the twenty-one-year-old Emperor. What they decided during five days of talk at Canterbury is not known, for even Henry's Chancellor, Thomas Cardinal Wolsey, was barred from some of the secret family sessions. It was, however, perfectly clear that Charles and Henry, with Catherine of Aragon's gentle approval, had agreed to agree on many things. One was to meet again as soon as possible after the Field of the Cloth of Gold. Another was the shrewd promise of Charles to help Wolsey—a man whose driving ambition matched his master's—to be the next Pope.

So now, even if Henry and Francis failed to come to any reasonable terms, Henry had a second string to his bow, an ace up his puffed sleeve.

Charles said a fond family farewell at Dover and set sail for his own Low Countries.

Shortly afterward, to the dull boom of cannon and the blare of trumpets, Henry boarded his own immense flagship *Henri-Grace-à-Dieu,* and she weighed anchor for the run across the narrow seas.

There is a fine picture by his court painter Hans Holbein which shows Henry on that day of days. Arms akimbo, legs broadly planted, he stands in the waist of the high-pooped ship. She bristles with cannon and is thronged with soldiers and courtiers. You can see how easily he dominates his subjects by his height and girth, and almost feel his burly strength.

It was some days before the two monarchs met. Their chief advisors—Bonnivet for France and Wolsey for England—had first of all to agree on many delicate matters of protocol and precedence. There was also the question of a treaty of friendship to be drafted.

Finally, on June 7, at the exact same hour, Francis I and Henry VIII each set out on horseback. The tent before which they were to meet was on English soil—a graceful concession of Francis's—but it was equidistant from the two encampments.

Both Kings were nervous. Each had his two most powerful noblemen in close attendance. Bourbon—the Constable of France—and Bonnivet—the High Admiral—rode just behind Francis. The Dukes of Norfolk and Suffolk were escort officers for Henry.

At a matching trot, the two resplendent monarchs approached the rendezvous.

Just at the last moment Henry's horse stumbled, which some thought a bad omen, but he quickly recovered. The Kings saluted each other while still mounted. Then, getting off their horses, they proceeded arm in arm into the tent.

"My dear brother and cousin," said Francis in that easy way of his, "I am come a long way and not without trouble to see you in person. I hope that you hold me for such as I am, ready to give you aid with the kingdoms and lordships that are in my power."

Henry's answer was somewhat less warm. "It is not your kingdoms or diverse possessions that I have regard for, but the soundness and loyal observance of the promises set down in the treaties between you and me."

Then he too yielded to the drama of the moment. "My eyes never beheld a prince who could be dearer to my heart, and I have crossed the seas at the extreme boundary of my kingdom to come and see you."

Inside, Bonnivet and Wolsey were waiting with the new treaty. One of the clauses concerned the future marriage of Henry's only child, the Princess Mary, and Francis's heir and namesake, the Dauphin. Since Mary was four at the time, and the Dauphin only two, it all seemed a little remote and unreal, but the proposed marriage was certainly a token of mutual good will. The good will was reinforced on Francis's part by an annual "token" payment of 100,000 livres.

Each having signed, the Kings drank a cup of wine together. Then they presented the ranking members of their courts. Henry was struck by Bourbon's almost-royal splendor of bearing and dress and his arrogant, sullen manner. Later

The Field of the Cloth of Gold

in the week, when he and Francis knew each other much better, he whispered: "If I had such a subject, he would not for long have his head on his shoulders!" Shades of tragedy-to-come, for the still-amiable English King would soon turn into a harsh and avid wielder of the executioner's axe.

Francis wanted his enormous party to be a success. But, in the dances and jousting and other forms of revelry that followed for a full sixteen days, there was a strong, swirling undercurrent of tension and distrust. The hard-bitten French veterans of the Italian wars did their best, and the English tried too. Yet somehow their hands never strayed very far from their sword hilts, and their eyes did not smile.

"The King of France," Fleuranges noted, "was mighty vexed at there being so little confidence in one another."

Being Francis, being bold, he took his own kind of action.

One morning very early he got up, told the first three people he met—two courtiers and a page—to follow him, and rode to the castle of Guines. He knew that Henry was spending the night there.

"Show me the King's chamber," he said cheerfully to the governor of the town.

"Sir, he is not yet awake," the astounded governor answered.

Francis found the chamber himself, knocked, and walked in. After his first astonishment, the rudely awakened King of England took the surprise visit very well indeed.

"You show me the great trust I ought to have in you," he said, declaring himself Francis's prisoner. He gave Francis a gold collar and Francis gave him a gold bracelet in return. When Henry climbed out of bed, Francis played valet to him, warming his shirt and helping him into it.

On the way back to Ardres, Francis was met by many of his staff who were worried over his safety. One was his friend Fleuranges.

"My dear master," said the Young Adventurer, "you are crazy to have done what you have done. Devil take him who counseled you."

"No one counseled me," said the King. "And there is not a soul in the kingdom who would have advised me to go."

Despite this openhearted gesture, the mistrust remained. One incident brought it very near to the surface. During a reception, when many people were about, Henry boisterously grabbed Francis by the collar.

"Brother, you shall wrestle with me!" he roared.

Taken by surprise in his turn, Francis instinctively fell back on his wrestler's skill. There was an ugly moment of twisting strain and then his majesty of England was sprawling full length on the carpet. His pale eyes seemed paler still as his face flushed with a dark red stain.

Now he was on his feet, squared off for another fall.

"Again," he grunted.

The two Queens stepped between them. Courtiers swarmed on all sides, passing it all off as a joke. So the incident was quickly over. Francis had used a trick hold to win a tactical victory, but it was one which did not much help him in the overall campaign.

There was one lighter moment when Queen Claude and

Queen Catherine met to take Communion together. Each waited politely to see who should have precedence in kissing the pax, the pax being the plate with Christ's image on it which figured in the Service at the time. Then, both laughing, they were suddenly kissing each other instead.

The first day of jousting had some good moments too, as we shall see.

Chapter 11

MEDIEVAL MOMENT

The lists are pleasantly located, with a slight rise on one side forming a natural gallery, and the dark forest behind. There are wooden balconies for the two Queens and their ladies, each balcony richly hung with silk and damask. Henry and Francis sit side by side under a brilliant canopy, well attended by squires and pages.

Francis gives the signal. Trumpets split the air with their silvery blast, and the heralds announce the first contest. It is to be four French knights against four English, in simultaneous single contests. Cheers and bursts of martial music greet the news.

Silence falls as the eight gleaming warriors take their places, with the English at the south end of the lists and the French at the north. The lists themselves—a continuous wooden barrier—run the length of the field between them.

The clarion sounds, shrill and clear, and the opponents spur toward each other at speed. They meet full tilt as lance shivers on shield or holds true. The ground trembles with the shock.

When the dust has cleared, the two Kings see that three of the four French knights have been unhorsed.

"By my faith, cousin," says Francis, "England hath the better of us."

The lone French survivor—Philip of Burgundy—and his English rival are each given a fresh lance. Again, they hurl themselves at eath other. Both reel in the saddle on impact. Then the Frenchman topples and goes down.

"You outweigh us," says Francis, "but in courage and spirit I would not exchange my men for any in your kingdom."

"And in obedience," Henry answers, "for at the command of their king they will flee an enemy."

The reference to the Battle of the Spurs seven years before could hardly have been more pointed. Francis bites his lips angrily as four more contestants ride to the two ends of the lists.

Clarion and clash and dust again, and this time all four Frenchmen are down.

"It is not our day," says Francis, half to himself, as the English stands go wild.

There is a pause, as if no more French challengers will appear. Then comes a long flourish of the herald's trumpet, and he intones a startling announcement: a new champion of the French cause challenges any or all of the victors in turn, or anyone else from the English ranks.

There is a sudden hush as the challenger rides slowly into the lists and stops before the pavilion of the two kings. He raises his visor in tribute and the French side roars in recognition.

"Bayard! Bayard!"

It is the knight without fear and above reproach, as many have guessed already by the superb way he sits his horse and the perfection of his armor—all steel and gold, like the man himself.

Three of the victorious Englishmen elect to challenge. Each goes down rather easily to the timing and horsemanship of Bayard.

"France first! France forever!" the French galleries yell and yell again.

After a brief rest, Bayard circles the lists on a fresh charger, lowering his lance in homage as he passes the Kings and their royal wives.

Now the herald's trumpet blows a long, defiant blast and all eyes turn instinctively to the English end of the lists. A big man in heavy armor comes thundering onto the field. At the sight of his famous fighting crest, thousands of English throats take up the cry: "Norfolk! Norfolk!"

The English nobleman rides straight to the place where Bayard sits his horse, relaxed but wary now. They both dismount and grasp each other's hands.

Norfolk speaks in his strong voice that can be heard by many: "Most noble Bayard, were it not for the honor of England I should hesitate to ride against the knight I most admire in the world. But this is England against France, not Norfolk against Bayard!"

Bayard's rich tones answer, matching Norfolk's knightly mood: "I am honored indeed that the leader of the English host should be willing to break a lance with me . . . for France then, and naught but friendship for Norfolk!"

The first run is a draw, with both men keeping their saddles, as lances shiver and horses are thrown back on their haunches by the jolting impact.

The second charge is even more furious. But Norfolk's horse swerves slightly toward the barrier so that the Englishman is thrown a shade off balance. Bayard's lance, perfectly placed on mid-shield, topples him. He slips slowly to the ground, and Bayard, off his horse in one swift motion, helps him to rise.

They leave the field arm in arm, to deafening cheers.

It is more in this chivalrous—already somewhat anachronistic—spirit that the Field of the Cloth of Gold festivities go on for the remaining time. But the underlying tension and mistrust are still there, and each King breathes a sigh of relief when it is all over.

With a final exchange of presents and mutual protestations of eternal friendship, they part at last on June 24.

For all its sunlit splendor, the Field of the Cloth of Gold was in one sense a twilight time. That chivalrous spirit, that surface courtesy, held much of the afterglow of the Middle Ages. It was also a mid-morning time, for the cynicism and political maneuvering in which the meeting was embedded anticipated the noontime years of the Renaissance.

The love of pageantry and display, which shone so splendidly there, was the contemporary quality, a trait shared equally by the waning age and the new.

(Among the many subjects that Francis and Henry discussed was the matter of a joint crusade against the Turk. As one historian put it, "Promises to take part in crusades always sat lightly on sixteenth-century princes." The truth was that the crusading spirit was as dead as the spirit of King Arthur and the quest for the Holy Grail.)

One thing was clear. Francis and Henry had taken each other's measure and neither liked what he saw. To Henry, the swaggering, mocking style of Francis was too much what he would have liked to possess himself. Francis for his part sensed the moody, vengeful, and jealous nature of the English King behind the red-gold good looks and under the bluff, good-king-Hal geniality.

Now, cherishing the fond hope that he had won an ally, Francis went straight to Amboise to rest and play awhile. Henry, in secret envy, headed northeast to Gravelines in Flanders to meet with his nephew and new co-conspirator, the Emperor Charles.

Chapter 12

THE GREAT CONSPIRATOR

It was obvious to all Europe that French King and Hapsburg Emperor were on a collision course. The next two years were spent in choosing up sides for the coming conflict, with Henry of England key man in this delicate and intricate game. He played his new role of odd-man-in very well indeed—supporting first one side and then the other, never quite showing his hand.

On October 23, 1520, Charles was crowned Holy Roman Emperor at Aachen in Germany—with the same iron crown that had served for the coronation of Charlemagne 720 years before.

A little over a year later, Pope Leo X died. Charles made a great public show of urging the College of Cardinals to elect Wolsey, as he had promised to do. At the same time, by secret letter, he urged certain key Cardinals *not* to do so. When a saintly Dutchman was chosen, and duly became Hadrian VI, Wolsey and his royal master received their first real lesson in the nimbleness and duplicity of Henry's Imperial nephew.

In January of 1521, Francis had had one of those accidents

which nearly change the course of history. During a snowball fight at Romorantin, he and some of his high-spirited comrades attacked the house of the Comte de Saint-Pol. Someone dropped a block of wood on the attackers. The log caught Francis on the side of the head, knocking him out. It took him two months to make a full recovery, while Europe held its breath. Fortunately the brain was not damaged, and his youth and strength pulled him through. To hide the long scar he grew a fuller beard, which in time became one of the most celebrated beards in history.

Louise of Savoy urged Francis to find and punish whoever had thrown the block of wood. His refusal was characteristic. "If I want to play the fool I must take what comes," he said.

In diplomacy he showed himself less boisterous and more mature. Although he knew that the clash with Charles was inevitable, Francis, like the Emperor, did not wish to be the first to plunge Europe into war. He did, however, encourage friends and neighbors to take the offensive. In the spring of 1522, one of his newer allies, Robert de La Marck, Prince of Sedan (and father of Fleuranges), invaded Luxembourg. Another near-henchman, André de Foix, overran Spanish-held Navarre. It was almost open warfare, and Charles saw it as such.

"Thank God," he said, "that I am not the first to commence the war, and that the King of France is pleased to make me greater than I am, for, in a little while, either I shall be a very poor Emperor or he will be a poor King of France."

The "little while" would last off and on for thirty-eight years and cost half a million lives. Neither Francis nor Charles would live to see the end of the bitter rivalry.

There was still some eleventh-hour temporizing. Francis forced La Marck to give up Luxembourg. André de Foix was beaten by the Spaniards in the battle of Ezquiros (June 30, 1521). Having won Navarre in fifteen days, he lost it again in one.

Now Imperial troops began to gather along the frontiers of Picardy in the north for what looked like more than mere defensive deployment.

Francis took reasonable measures in all the sensitive areas. He gave himself the responsibility for the defense of Burgundy to the east; he sent Bonnivet to the Spanish border; he ordered Lautrec to place the duchy of Milan in a state of readiness. More important for the moment, he chose the Duke of Alençon and Charles of Bourbon to defend the threatened northern frontiers. This was all very well, except that the command of the advance guard there fell to Alençon, whose main qualification was that he was the husband of Marguerite of Angoulême.

Alençon was in fact a bit ridiculous. He was a man given to commanding rear guards and baggage trains. He had been last across the Alps in 1515 and the left wing, which he commanded, at Melegnano had almost been turned. During one of the Christmas festivities at Blois, his horse had stumbled and he broke his arm, and at the Field of the Cloth of Gold his tent caught fire. Hardly a man to raise above the fierce, black-browed Constable of France!

Charles of Bourbon brooded. He had, in fact, been brooding for some time, for he was a proud man who hoarded insults and collected injuries, both real and imagined.

As far back as the time of Louis XII—when Bourbon was winning his long spurs in many battles—the King was well aware of his sullen nature as well as his bravery. "I wish," he said, "that he had a more open, gayer, less taciturn spirit; stagnant water affrights me."

In Francis's time, the problem of Charles of Bourbon was a residual one, left over from when the great nobles were forever challenging the power of the monarchy. He was the last of the great feudal paladins. All the others had been either brought to heel or killed off.

One of the reasons why he was so dangerous was that his lands were in the heartland of France. Besides his great Bourbon dukedom, he was Duke of Dauphiné, of Auvergne, and of Châtellerault. He was also Count of Clermont and Montpensier (where he was born) and Vicomte of Carlat and Murat. He ruled these rich provinces and counties like a monarch, collecting taxes and administering justice. Although he paid homage to Francis and served him in time of war, he acted in all else—including the magnificence of his own court at Moulins—like an equal rather than a subject.

Francis knew that before he could really make war on the Emperor he would have to settle this matter of Charles of Bourbon. He knew it, but he did not like it. His sanguine, too-trusting nature shrank from drastic action against a soldier whose prowess he admired and a kinsman whose friendship he would have liked.

In 1517 the King went to Moulins for the christening of Charles's first son. He was amazed and disturbed by the size of the court. To his trained eyes, the five hundred gentlemen in attendance on the duke seemed as haughty and hardbitten as their master.

One day Francis and Charles of Bourbon rode past Bonnivet's splendid new castle of Neuville, which was in the vicinity of Châtellerault.

"What do you think of it?" Francis asked.

"I think, Sire," replied Bourbon, "that the cage is too big for the bird."

"You are jealous!"

"Can Your Majesty believe that I am jealous of a gentleman whose ancestors were happy to be squires of mine?"

The truth of course was that Bourbon was the caged bird and that he was jealous as well. It was the bird rather than the cage that had grown too big. Brave, cheerful Bonnivet, Francis's boon companion since childhood, was never any trouble at all.

Francis's own motives in making Bourbon Constable of France were mixed. To honor his valor, *certainly*. To bribe him to be faithful, *perhaps*. To keep him where he could watch him, *perhaps again*. To please his mother, who was in love with Bourbon, *very likely*.

Francis also gave Bourbon the coveted collar of the Order of St. Michael. Both honors were for life, but the office of Constable was the dangerous one, for it carried with it—in theory, at least—command of the armies of France. Some said that half the armed forces were waiting to do whatever Bourbon ordered.

During the years after Melegnano, Bourbon made several enemies in high places. One was Chancellor Duprat, whom he treated like a servant. Another was Louise of Savoy. It seems that the Queen Mother first fell in love with him when he was sixteen and she was thirty. Later she made a fairly obvious proposal of marriage, which he brutally rejected. By 1521, she too was his mortal enemy.

Like almost everyone else, Bourbon is supposed to have been in love with Marguerite of Angoulême. Restlessly unhappy in her marriage to the absurd Alençon, she may well have been dazzled by the Constable's arrogance and smoldering pride. But most of the evidence indicates that her heart was permanently absorbed in that passionate tenderness of hers for her brother the King.

(Bonnivet, too, was in love with Marguerite. We know this on firmer grounds, for she tells it herself in her collection of thinly disguised stories called the *Heptameron*. Encouraged by Louise of Savoy, who was as disappointed in Alençon as Marguerite herself was, he took direct action. One night at Amboise, after she was asleep, he entered her room by a secret door and tried to make love to her. She fought him tooth and nail—a rare experience for the High Admiral of France—and raised the whole household by her screams. His face streaming with blood, Bonnivet fled to safer ground.)

At Francis's incomparable Court . . . at the Field of the Cloth of Gold . . . at his own near-royal city of Moulins,

Bourbon cut a splendid figure. He loved gold so much that
he was never served at table with any other metal. From
plates to goblets, from mirrors to spurs, all was gold. He
himself glittered with diamonds and other precious stones.
Far from making him seem effeminate, they added to the
fascination of his somber and haughty bearing.

As early as 1519, he was being wooed by both Charles
V and Henry VIII. That was the year in which his only
son died at the age of three, a tragedy which contributed to
his own dark destiny.

It was also clear that Bourbon's frail little wife Suzanne
was not long for this world. Suzanne was the daughter of
the famous Anne of France, daughter in her turn of Louis XI.
(During the minority of Charles VIII, Anne had been a
brilliant Regent of France.)

At their marriage, Suzanne brought Bourbon many of the
castles and towns and broad acres that he now ruled.

Suzanne died in 1521, leaving all her holdings to her
husband. Urged on by Louise of Savoy, who claimed them
for herself as Anne of France's niece, the King promptly
confiscated these lands. So began an interminable lawsuit
that, more than any other event, propelled Bourbon toward
treason.

It was true that he already had cause to be bitter. The
fact that he had been replaced as governor of Milan by the
much less able Lautrec, and later given a humiliating command under Alençon, had rankled. Now the threat to his
property was too much for his proud spirit.

His secret negotiations with Henry and the Emperor went

into high gear. One of the subjects discussed was a three-pronged invasion of France; another was the possibility of Bourbon's marrying Charles's sister Eleanor.

Such bold actions as the waylaying and imprisonment of Francis, the return of Burgundy to the Hapsburgs, and the carving of a whole kingdom for Bourbon out of the heartland and southern flank of France were also items on the agenda. Henry would have broad lands to add to his toe hold in the north and perhaps even the title of King of France, which he said belonged to him anyway from the dim past.

Although the emissaries of Emperor, King, and duke met in deep secrecy, these talks did not go unnoticed, for Bourbon was not, ever, a cautious man. With that trick of understatement of his, Fleuranges observed that "in the spring of 1523, Monsieur de Bourbon, Constable of France, did not take the pleasure he should have in his office."

In March of that same year, Bourbon was at the Louvre, having an audience with Queen Claude, who in her gentle way understood this driving and driven man.

Francis burst in. "Well, is it true that you are getting married?" he asked Bourbon point-blank.

"No, Sire."

"I know it, I am sure of it. I know all about your dealing with the Emperor! Just be sure to remember what I am saying now."

"Sire, you threaten me. I do not deserve to be treated like this."

Shortly afterwards, Bourbon left the palace, with so powerful an escort that no one dared to stop him.

It was at about this time that Charles of Bourbon changed

Charles of Bourbon, drawing from the school of Clouet

his family's proud motto, *Espérance,* to a more ominous one, *Tout Mon Espoir Est dans le Fer.* The simple word for "hope" became a challenge and a cry: "All My Hope Is in the Sword." At the same time he took a flying stag as his crest.

He himself was almost on the run.

The year before, something had happened in Italy which sharpened the tensions in France and brought all-out war nearer than ever. Lautrec was beaten by the Imperial forces at the battle of La Bicoque (April 27, 1522). Although some strong points remained in French hands, almost all the duchy of Milan was lost. When Lautrec reported back to Francis at Lyons, he found the King bitter and angry. Lautrec protested.

"Why shouldn't I be angry?" said Francis. "You lost me my great duchy."

"It was not I who lost it," said Lautrec. "It was Your Majesty." He went on to say that the money to pay his Swiss mercenaries had never come through.

"I sent you the 400,000 crowns when you asked for them," Francis said.

"I received the letters in which Your Majesty notified me about this money, but the money never."

It developed that Jacques de Beaune, Baron of Semblançay, the trusted Superintendent General of Finance, had turned the money over to Louise of Savoy at her urgent request. He had been about to obey the King's orders to send it to Lautrec and had assumed that Louise would do so.

Unpaid and unhappy, the Swiss troops had forced Lautrec into a premature battle, in the hope of booty.

Francis went roaring into Louise's rooms, furiously angry, and accused her of losing him Milan. Startled, she tried to justify herself, saying that it was money that had long been due her. But Francis could never be angry with her for long. The real scar was Louise's growing hatred of Semblançay for his candor in telling about the 400,000 crowns. Thinking that he was her man like so many other court officials, she had hoped that he would help her to confuse the issue, not to clarify it. Five years later, it would cost him his life.

Francis now made one more try to keep Bourbon from going over to the enemy.

With a strong troop of archers and foot soldiers in attendance, he hurried to Moulins for a confrontation with Bourbon. The Constable claimed that he was ill, but the King went directly to his bedroom. He found the Constable in bed. Fleuranges and others have recorded what happened at the interview.

"Monsieur de Bourbon," said Francis, "I have been warned that you are having dealings with the Emperor and the English. I pray you if it is true to tell me so, and I pardon you with all my heart—and don't worry, I will always be your friend."

"Sire, those who have warned you are false liars, for I am your good subject and loyal servant."

Francis then said he planned to have Bourbon come with him to Italy for the start of the new campaign there.

"Would you come with me willingly?" the King asked.
"Not only to Italy but to the end of the world."

Even at this eleventh hour, there was something in Bourbon's proud spirit that made an admission of treason impossible—that may even have hoped that he was not lost beyond recall.

Nevertheless, he pleaded illness, promising he would join Francis in Italy as soon as his doctors said he could bear the motion of a litter.

The King went away satisfied, although his bolder advisors urged him to arrest Bourbon on the spot.

The cat-and-mouse game lasted another three weeks. Francis, at Lyons, was determined not to leave for Italy without the Constable, and the Constable was determined to be just ill enough so that Francis would go without him.

Then, suddenly much improved in health, Bourbon left Moulins and rode to his strong, isolated castle of Chantelle, where he felt much safer.

Francis ordered his arrest at last.

Hearing that royal troops were about to surround the castle, Bourbon and a few chosen comrades slipped away by night. One of the comrades was a wiry soldier called Pompérant, who was his most faithful friend.

That was in early September. For several months the greatest lord of the realm led the life of a fugitive. He changed his disguise often, traveled only by back roads and at night. Sometimes, as he worked east, he would fall in with royal troops on their way to Italy.

At one point, acting as valet to Pompérant, he crossed the Rhône on a flat barge with some of Francis's veterans.

They all knew Pompérant and waved cheerfully, thinking he too was bound for Italy. But they failed to recognize the tall man in the black hat and black linen cloak.

Later, at an inn in a village near the Rhône, the innkeeper's wife spotted Pompérant.

"Are you not one of those who has been playing the fool with M. de Bourbon?" she asked jokingly.

"Not I," he replied. "But I would give all I have to be in his company."

Finally, one dark November night, Bourbon and Pompérant reached Imperial territory in Franche-Comté. When Francis learned of his escape, he sent a messenger offering a full pardon and the return of all the confiscated lands if the duke would come back.

"It is too late," Bourbon answered.

The King's messenger then asked him to surrender the sword of the Constable and the collar of the Order of St. Michael.

"You will tell the King," said Bourbon, "that he took from me the sword of the Constable on the day that he took from me the command of the advance guard to give it to M. d'Alençon. As for the collar of his Order, you will find it at Chantelle, under the pillow of my bed."

Francis's men found the golden collar of St. Michael with its eight-pointed cross exactly where the Constable had said it was. But Charles of Bourbon had crossed his own sad Rubicon at last. The great bird had flown his cage forever.

$\mathcal{C}$hapter 13

A   T E M P E R E D   J U S T I C E

Charles of Bourbon was a great conspirator, but his was not a great conspiracy. Very few of his henchmen followed him into exile. Just about all that he brought his new master was his sword, the gold coins sewn into the lining of his jacket, and the faithful Pompérant. The French army never rose to follow; the nobles who had favored his cause simply went to cover and hoped that their near-treason would pass unnoticed.

The truth was that France was sick to death of arrogant noblemen like Bourbon. Among the people of the thriving cities and towns—the doctors, bankers, and lawyers, the artisans and craftsmen, whose ranks and voice were growing by the year—a new spirit of nationalism was forming. They wanted prestige for their country, and they recognized that a strong central authority was the best way to attain it. They liked how Francis went about his royal duties, and they liked his style and dash.

Early in his reign, the King had shown the Paris Parlement that he intended to be master. The Parlement was bitterly opposed to the Concordat that Francis made with

Pope Leo in 1516. Knowing very well that the Concordat would add greatly to the royal power (especially in the matter of placing all the high ecclesiastical appointments in the King's hands), the members tried to block it.

While the Parlement's main role had always been the administering of justice, its approval was required for most royal statutes and edicts. This fact was interpreted by its members as implying some lawmaking responsibilities.

Francis sent a crisp and unmistakable message: "I will not permit that there be more than one King in France. There will not be a Senate here as in Venice which lays down its laws for the prince. Parlement's mission is to render justice and not to busy itself with other things. I wish and demand that the Concordat be enregistered."

Grudgingly, the Parlement bowed to the authentic voice of the master.

This was something new. Louis XII had been an easygoing, not-very-royal king. Like his predecessors, he was simply the first among many great nobles of ancient family who considered themselves his "peers" or equals. By contrast, Francis was the first king to rule *du bon plaisir,* in that his will, his pleasure, was above the law, and in a fair way of quickly becoming law if he so desired.

Now Francis moved vigorously to stamp out any embers of conspiracy. With the country still in danger of invasion from Bourbon's allies, an example had to be made. The logical man was Jean de Poitiers, Lord of Saint-Vallier, who had been a party to the signing of Bourbon's treaty with

Charles V. Dutifully enough, the Paris Parlement carried out the trial. Nor was there any real question of his guilt. On January 16, 1524, he was condemned to be beheaded.

His beautiful daughter Diane de Poitiers, one of the rising stars of the royal Court, begged the King to save his life. So did many others. Merciful by nature, Francis still felt that a public lesson was necessary.

The aged Saint-Vallier was taken trembling from his prison in the Conciergerie. His harsh sentence was read to him at the Palais de Justice. Then, tied like a parcel to a soldier on horseback, he was carried to the Place de Grève, where public executions were held. Before a dense crowd, he knelt on the scaffold, neck bared for the headsman's great two-handed sword.

The scene froze, as if time itself had stopped.

The masked headsman stood by with arms folded. Saint-Vallier prayed. He begged the executioner to get on with his business. The crowd stirred restlessly.

Suddenly a messenger on horseback pushed his way through.

"The King's reprieve!" he shouted, waving a piece of parchment. He climbed up on the scaffold and read the royal decree in a loud voice. It commuted the death sentence to life imprisonment and perpetual disgrace.

In his own theatrical way, Francis had tempered justice with mercy.

Chapter 14

A SYMBOLIC DEATH

At about the time of Bourbon's defection, Pope Hadrian VI cast his lot with the Emperor Charles (whose tutor he had once been). When Francis heard the news, he made one of those bravura remarks of his. "All Europe is in league against me," he cried. "So much the better, I will face all Europe."

With Bourbon's flight and treason, the concerted attacks against France did gain some momentum. Even though Charles V was chronically short of money, and Henry VIII's support was quicksilver only, the fiery Constable was able to prod both into action. A mixed English–Flemish force of 30,000 men invaded Picardy from the north. A smaller army of German *Landsknechts* attacked Champagne from the east, while in the south the Constable of Castille, one of the Emperor's most experienced lieutenants, crossed the Pyrenees and laid siege to Bayonne.

Francis was at his best in these extreme situations. Using the interior lines of communication of a whole nation under siege, he set up headquarters at Lyons and took steps to isolate and reduce the three-pronged threat. Choosing his captains well, he gave them good support and a free hand.

The young Count Claude of Guise, first famous member of that colorful, ambitious clan, beat the Germans in Champagne and then put them completely to rout as they retreated into Lorraine.

Two of Francis's veteran commanders, La Trémoille and Lautrec, were successful to the north and south. Operating in Picardy, where he knew every valley and creek and crenelated strong point, La Trémoille outwitted and exhausted the halfhearted English–Flemish expeditionary force. The invaders made a perfunctory pass at Paris and then, as the bitter winter set in, withdrew.

In the south, Lautrec's troops moved with speed and vigor, forcing the Constable of Castille to raise the siege of Bayonne and retreat back across the Pyrenees.

The fourth theater of operations was Italy, that perennial cockpit of dynastic wars. Francis made the mistake of putting Bonnivet in command of his campaign to recapture the duchy of Milan.

Big and solid, with an aquiline nose and a slight beard, Bonnivet was, as we know, a well-liked man. Jean Giono, one of France's great modern writers, said that "he made love like war and war like love." Giono also noted that today he would be the cheerful fellow "who knows the names of all the headwaiters."

Boon companion of the monarch, brave as a mountain lion, he didn't have a ray of sense. Quite aware of this, Francis gave him the strongest supporting cast he could muster: men like the Comte de Saint-Pol, Marshal La Palice, and the incomparable Chevalier Bayard.

Francis also made sure that Bonnivet had a mettlesome army, for Italy was as ever the land that his warrior heart desired most.

At first, in the early months of 1524, all went well. The High Admiral moved briskly to lay siege to the city of Milan. But once there he never could quite decide what he wanted to do next, and his hesitations and blunders gave Charles V time to organize his defense. In the area, the Emperor was fortunate in having three first-class commanders who would serve him brilliantly: the Marquis of Pescara, Charles de Lannoy (Viceroy of Naples)—and Charles of Bourbon.

For a while Charles V had had misgivings about trusting a traitor like Bourbon with a field command. There was always the chance that such a strong, self-willed man might suffer remorse, might even repent his treason. The Emperor finally made up his mind to take a chance. He appointed Bourbon his lieutenant general in Italy. This decision, perhaps more than anything else except Bonnivet's incompetence, sealed the fate of the French expeditionary force.

Bad luck began to dog the French. Their supplies ran out. Much-needed Swiss reinforcements were delayed. On April 30, 1524, Bonnivet was severely wounded and had to turn over his command to Saint-Pol and Bayard. The siege of Milan by then had become a retreat from Milan.

That day, Bayard as usual was counter-attacking, at the exact spot where the Imperial troops were pressing the hardest. In the midst of a gallant cavalry charge, he was struck by a shot from a sniper's arquebus. The bullet broke his lower spine.

"My God," he cried, "I am dead." He held up his sword and kissed the hilt as if it were a cross. Deathly pale, he continued to cling to his saddlebow, until one of his squires helped him dismount and then placed him under a tree with his face to the enemy.

The squire wept, and the chevalier did his best to console him.

"Leave off thy mourning," he said. "It is God's will to take me out of this world; by His Grace I have lived long therein, and have received blessings and honors more than my due." Bayard then begged his squire not to try to move him, for he knew that he was beyond help.

Hearing that Bayard was wounded, Charles of Bourbon came and stood before the stricken knight. Bourbon was in full armor except that his bowed head was bare.

There is something legendary about the scene which ensued, with dying hero and somber traitor brought face to face by the winds of chance and the misfortunes of war.

A chronicle of the time catches this mythical quality very well indeed:

And the Constable said to the aforesaid Bayard that he had great pity for him, seeing him in so sad a state for a knight of such prowess. To this the Captain Bayard made response: "Monsieur, there is no need to pity me, for I die an honest man. But I have pity for you to see you serving thus, against your prince and your country and your oath." And shortly thereafter the said Bayard gave up the ghost.

Bourbon left the scene without saying another word.

Bayard actually lingered for two or three hours more. A priest was found and he made his confession. His squire and several others refused to leave his side. The Marquis of Pescara rode up to pay sad tribute to the prowess of the fallen foe.

The knight without fear and above reproach died at last, as calmly and nobly as he had lived.

His death marked the passing of all that was best in the waning age of chivalry. It was symbolic—and ironic too— that the man whose matchless fame had been won by sword and lance should be killed by a sniper's bullet. Modern warfare, fought with rifles, handguns, and cannon, was fast replacing medieval war.

Friend and foe mourned the chevalier equally, knowing that the European world was a grimmer place with his passing. For two days he lay in state in an Italian church, by order of the chiefs of the Imperial army. Then, with all the honors of war, his body was returned to his grieving comrades.

Sadly, in fair order, Bonnivet's battered army withdrew toward the frontiers of France.

Chapter 15

AN ILL-FATED MISTRESS, A SIEGE GONE SOUR

Sometime in that same spring of 1524, Francis took a new mistress. She was a slim, fair, frizzy-haired girl called Anne de Pisseleu de Heilly, and she had a far more agreeable disposition than Françoise de Châteaubriant. The darkly beautiful Françoise had begun to grow tiresome, and not just to the King. She demanded too much worship from everyone. In marked contrast to the self-effacing Queen Claude herself, she put on too many queenly airs.

Needless to say, the new romance was engineered and endorsed by Louise of Savoy and Marguerite of Angoulême, who always and always had the King's best interests at heart.

Françoise did not go without a struggle. She warned her royal lover against blond, blue-eyed women—on the grounds that, being dark himself, he had more in common with dark beauties. But Francis had fallen very much in love with the calm, clear Anne de Pisseleu de Heilly.

She came from an old family in Picardy. Pisseleu was originally *pire que loup,* for one of her medieval ancestors had been worse than a wolf on the field of battle. Anne was less fiery. In due course Francis found a complacent husband for her, and created him Duc d'Étampes. It is as

Duchesse d'Étampes, and Francis's official mistress for the twenty-three remaining years of his life, that Anne has her place in history.

Poor stormy Françoise! She loitered around the edges of the Court for a while and then retired to her husband's gaunt castle in Brittany, to brood over her lost love. Once, at Anne d'Étampes's urging, Francis wrote her with an odd request. He asked her to return all the gold rings and bracelets that he had given her. Many of them were inscribed with tender words and phrases that the King, in his rather offhand way, thought would be just as pleasing to Anne.

Françoise told the King's messenger to come back in three days. She took to her bed to ponder the request. When the messenger came back, she had not only reached a decision but taken spirited action: she returned the golden trove all right, but first of all she had had a jeweler melt down the rings and bracelets.

"Go," she said to the messenger, "take these to the King and tell him that since it pleased him to call back that which he gave me so liberally, I send it back to him in ingots of gold. And as for the devices and inscriptions, I have so well imprinted them and placed them in order in my thoughts— and hold them so dear—that I cannot allow anyone to enjoy them and have pleasure from them but me."

Louise of Savoy thought this insolent, and was furious. Francis himself was amused and a little touched.

"Take the whole lot back to her," he said. "What I was doing was not for the value but for the love of the inscriptions. Since she has now caused them to be lost in this way, I don't want any of the gold, and so send it back. She has

Anne de Pisseleu, Duchesse d'Étampes,
portrait by Corneille de Lyon

shown in this matter more generosity and courage than one would have thought could come from a woman."

As time passed, Françoise became more and more a recluse. There is a terrible story, half legend perhaps, concerning her end. It seemed that her husband, Jean de Laval, had also been brooding. Although he had taken her infidelity in stride, and allowed himself to be made Duc de Châteaubriant to ensure his tacit approval of it, he had never forgiven her.

One dark night he came to her room in a lonely tower of his castle, with two of his lackeys to attend and assist him.

She faced him calmly enough.

"Madam," he said, "your time has come."

He signaled to his men. They drew their daggers. He stood by with crossed arms while they stabbed her to death.

The official report was that Françoise had died in bed. No one ever brought the duke to justice. In the fast-breaking events of those days and months, as history hurtled on, poor Françoise had become just a gusty memory.

The winter of 1523 had brought Francis several strokes of luck which meant that all Europe was no longer against him. Hadrian VI died and the newly chosen Pope, Giulio de' Medici—who took the name of Clement VII—was more inclined to be neutral than his predecessor. By trying to please everyone, he ended pleasing no one. But for the moment Francis was hemmed in by one less enemy.

Another somewhat surprising new friend was Andrea Doria, the famous Genoese admiral, who had already steered his city-state through many troubled seas. A man so formidable that, as one contemporary remarked, "even the sea was afraid of him," he had quarreled with the Emperor. He indicated that he would actively support Francis in Italy and elsewhere.

Elsewhere came first. For on July 1, 1524, Charles of Bourbon invaded France. Aflame for action, he led a mixed army of over 20,000 men—Germans, Italians, and Spaniards —into Provence. Andrea Doria manhandled the accompanying Imperial fleet, but the land forces took town after town, encountering only token resistance.

Having captured Vence, Antibes, Cannes, and Aix-en-Provence—where the city magistrates obligingly swore him in as Count of Provence—Bourbon laid siege to Marseilles.

He himself had wanted to press straight up the Rhône for Lyons and then to Paris. But the Marquis of Pescara and the other Spanish generals in his polyglot army had their orders: Charles V needed the great seaport city as the connecting link between his Italian and Spanish lands.

Bourbon agreed in his flamboyant way. "Three cannon shots," he said, "will amaze the good citizens so much that they will come, halters around their necks, bringing me the keys of the city."

The overall plot was for Henry VIII to knife down simultaneously from the north, but this time the English sovereign simply dragged his feet.

Marseilles proved a tougher nut to crack than expected. There were 9,000 militia there, and an aroused population determined to hold out at all costs against the French arch-traitor and his new allies.

Bourbon poured 800 stone and iron cannon balls into the city. He also made some sharp forays, which the defenders turned back with accurate fire by cannon and arquebus.

On September 7, Bourbon's great siege guns succeeded in opening a jagged breach in the half-ruined walls. He was about to order an all-out assault when he saw something that gave him pause: behind the rampart that had crumbled there was a new rampart of earth and wood and stone.

Working at night, with the spirited help of the women of Marseilles, the defenders had leveled a section of the city. This gave them the material for the new wall and a cleared space before it, which they could sweep with their own fire.

The fiery Bourbon still wanted to attack. His Spanish officers, however, were less enthusiastic. The fact was that they cared very little for a man who was even more arrogant than they were themselves. They rather enjoyed his embarrassment over the strong resistance.

Some days passed. One morning, when Pescara was hearing mass in his tent, a cannon ball fired from the ramparts killed the officiating priest and two of Pescara's staff.

Bourbon rushed over. "What was that?" he cried.

"That was the good people of Marseilles bringing you the keys of the city," Pescara replied.

On September 24, a probing attack through the breach failed, with heavy casualties. Noting that a wide ditch had now been dug before the new rampart, Pescara urged Bourbon to make no more vain assaults.

"The table is beautifully laid," he said. "If you want to sup tonight in paradise, hurry up. If not, follow me to Italy, which has no one to defend it and is going to be invaded."

There was also news from the north. Francis, with a big army, was marching at speed to relieve Marseilles. Marshal La Palice and the advance guard were only ten miles away.

Bourbon knew when to cut his losses. In cold anger, he raised the siege. On September 28, with La Palice in hot pursuit, he took the bitter road back to Italy.

Francis had said goodbye to Queen Claude at Amboise in July. She was far from well. Seven children in eight years, and a recent attack of pleurisy, had exhausted her. The doctors said she might live until fall, but Francis had his own sense of foreboding.

He wept after leaving her.

"If I could buy her life with mine, I would do it with all my heart," he said to Marguerite when she tried to console him. "Never could I have believed that the bond of marriage enjoined by God would be so firm and difficult to break."

Claude died on July 26, when Francis was already moving south with his army. And all France mourned the gentle Queen.

Both Louise and Marguerite took Francis's warlike plans very hard indeed. Knowing well that his ultimate goal was Italy, they tried to dissuade him.

Louise put her own feelings into a remarkable poem. It opens with these lines:

> *There is but one heart, one mind, one thought*
> *'Twixt you and me, in love forever . . .*

And it closes on the same theme, with a shortened line that is like a catch in the throat:

> *Without constraint or counter-thought*
> *There is but one heart.*

Louise wrote Francis, begging him to meet her on important matters. His reply was to send her the final papers making her Regent in his absence, as he had done before.

On his way to relieve Marseilles, Francis came to the town of Manosque, above Aix-en-Provence. He was greeted there by the pretty daughter of a prosperous burgher, chosen to present him the keys of the little town. Francis looked and, liking, looked again. He made it quite clear, in that half mocking way of his, that he was interested. That evening the girl scarred her face with a vapor of burning sulphur, destroying the beauty that had made her too pleasing to the King.

He sighed—and rode on.

This episode was most unusual in times when a handsome monarch was used to having his own way. All his life Francis would react reflexively to a pretty face. The truth was—the real problem, if you will—that he never cared for anyone, even Françoise or Anne, as much as he cared for Louise and for Marguerite.

Still, there were times when a loving mother and a doting sister were too much of a muchness. Not a little relieved to be caught up again in the glorious uncertainties of war, Francis marched south by east in Bourbon's track.

By mid-October, he had crossed the Alps. Now he was in enemy territory and the whole game was once again in hazard.

Chapter 16

THE BOULDER IN
THE LOMBARD PLAIN

The great city of Milan was a grim, sad place that fall of 1524. Plague-ridden, half ruined from many sieges, it was no longer worth defending or capturing. On the run now, Bourbon fled past it without pausing. He needed time to regroup his disheartened forces and to raise more funds. Besides, he wanted to put plenty of space between himself and the splendid new French army.

On his own way down into Lombardy, Francis spent two or three nights with his slippery uncle, the Duke of Savoy. Louise's brother received him cordially but neglected to mention that he had already pledged gold and jewels to help the arch-enemy, Charles of Bourbon.

Francis quickly reached the husk of the city. Outside Milan's crumbling and polluted walls, he called a council of war to decide what to do. He had 40,000 troops, the best artillery in Europe, good supply lines, and for once enough money to pay the professional soldiers for months to come. *So what next?*

All Francis's top captains and colonels and knights-in-arms were present. (Colonel was a new, exalted rank, deriving from *couronne:* a coronel or colonel was appointed by the *crown* itself.)

Bonnivet was there of course, the handsomest, most agreeable of warriors. So was Fleuranges, with his bravery and his irony. Those three hard-bitten commanders—La Palice, Lautrec, and La Trémoille—were very much there. Galiot de Genouillac was there too, fastidious about his guns, a little surly like all artillerymen because he felt he had more responsibility than chance of glory. Anne of Montmorency was there, less reckless than many, a hard-working nobleman with a firm mouth and good, steady eyes. The Comte de Saint-Pol was there, and the Bastard of Savoy, Francis's uncle, who, like Francis, loved a good battle. So was Clément Marot the poet, who had been named the King's *varlet de chambre,* and whose nimble verses pleased his new master very much indeed. And of course Alençon was there, duller than ever.

Only Bayard was missing among those who were really close to the King. Missing and greatly missed, for his had been the ultimate voice of valor and good sense.

La Trémoille and La Palice—Marshals of France both—wanted Francis to press forward in pursuit of the disorganized Imperial army. But Bonnivet urged him to capture Pavia first. This well-fortified second city of the duchy sat like a big boulder in the Lombard plain. Whoever held it would hold the duchy, Bonnivet said.

Francis never could resist Bonnivet's advice, and so he overruled the cooler heads of the two marshals. Twenty days after setting out from Aix, he appeared before Pavia and proceeded to deploy his army within cannon shot of its biscuit-colored walls.

When the Marquis of Pescara heard the news, he rejoiced. "We were vanquished," he said. "A little while now and we shall be vanquishers."

The siege lasted from October to late February. A Spanish captain called Antonio de Leyva defended the city with great spirit. Tiny, with his hands "the size of oyster forks," he was so lame he had to be carried about in a basket. But he gave Francis a dose of his own Marseilles medicine, proving that 6,000 men could stop six or seven times as many besiegers in their tracks, when walls and morale were high. His Swiss and Spanish soldiers were reduced to eating mice, after the mules and dogs gave out. After the money ran out, de Leyva melted down all the gold ornaments in the churches and struck his own crude coins to pay the men.

Francis was so confident that the city would surrender that he sent 10,000 of his army south under his Scottish friend the Duke of Albany. Albany was to capture that other will-o'-the-wisp, the Kingdom of Naples, or at least create a diversion there. Meanwhile, Francis himself settled in a walled park called Montebello. The park was on high ground on the outskirts of the beleaguered city. As a precaution against any sudden foray or surprise attack, the King had earthworks dug around its perimeter. Then, well-entrenched and well-provisioned, he waited for the Pavian plum to fall.

In December the weather turned bitterly cold. It was one of the worst winters anyone could remember. The river Po froze over, melted a little, froze again. The long thin lines of poplars shivered across the Lombard plain. The tall columns of smoke rising from farm and village seemed frozen in the pale-blue sky.

There was more on the march than poplars that winter, more columns than smoke columns in the great plain. Supplies, reinforcements, endless letters from Louise of Savoy, came swiftly through from France. Fast couriers left Montebello almost daily with news and instructions for the Regent.

In January, some days ahead of the fact itself, the word reached the invaders: Bourbon and Lannoy and Pescara with a brand-new army were marching to relieve Antonio de Leyva.

What Pescara foresaw so clearly had happened. Francis had stubbed his toe on the rock in the plain. By undertaking the long siege, he gave Charles of Bourbon the needed breathing spell.

Bourbon acted with great energy. Leaving his remnant of an army, traveling fast and light, he went to Savoy and Germany for funds and fresh troops. Impressed with his drive and zeal, the Duke of Savoy made good his promise of financial help. Charles V's lieutenants in Germany came up with both men and money, for this Bourbon was a hard man to deny. (As for the Emperor himself, he was in seclusion in Spain. But he was watching everything and making all the big decisions.)

Moving with the notable slowness of legal bodies, the Parlement of Paris finally got around to confiscating Bourbon's vast lands. They were given to the crown, all the turreted cities and rich rolling counties that the Constable had loved so well. Now the man-who-would-be-king had only his soldiers for subjects, and the only country he had was his armed camp. As for the soldiers, they worshipped their leader and trusted him to lead them to gold and glory.

Those two skeptical lieutenants of Bourbon's, Pescara and Lannoy, could not fail to be impressed by what Bourbon had done. They knew well that the new Imperial army, added to de Leyva's forces at Pavia, was roughly equivalent to Francis's total strength. Without question, the French artillery was better, and so was their heavy cavalry. But the Spanish commanders had created a new, secret instrument of war: they had trained 1,500 riflemen to shoot at close quarters, reload quickly behind a protective screen of pikemen, and shoot again.

Bourbon and Lannoy and Pescara knew, too, that the French had grown fat and indolent in winter quarters. Early in the siege they had shown some initiative. In November they had actually tried to dam the river Ticino above the city. This was Alençon's idea, in one of his better moments, and it had its points. The hard-pressed city would be deprived of most of its water, and the exposed river bed would be a good vantage point for attack, since the river washed the weak point in the city walls.

The idea became another of the luckless Alençon's failures. For late-autumn rains made the Ticino rise. The swollen river burst through the improvised dam of wood and earth, and the big wooden planks went twisting downstream to the Po some miles below the city.

A little too complacent, a little too content to await the inevitable surrender of the city, the French dug themselves in. That was how matters stood in late January when Bourbon's buoyant new army came marching across the plain, pikes and gun barrels and breastplates gleaming in the pale winter sunlight.

Bourbon pitched camp very close to Francis's. In effect, he now laid siege to the French army which was laying siege to Pavia. For nearly four weeks the two armies eyed each other warily.

The long-burning fuse was nearing the powder keg. The stage was set for one of the decisive battles of history.

Chapter 17

"ALL IS LOST SAVE HONOR"

It was the best of battles. It was the worst of battles. It was the first contest of one kind, and the last of another. It was a night of murk and fog, and a morning of cannonades and bugles. In its brief span there was much glory and the death of many paladins.

It is known to history as the Battle of Pavia.

Each side held its own council of war to decide whether to attack or not. As usual, there was sharp disagreement in the French camp. Those veteran commanders, La Palice and La Trémoille, pointed out to Francis that he held a strong defensive position in the park of Montebello. All he really had to do was wait a few more days for the surrender of the starving city. There were also reliable reports that the Imperial army itself was short of food and cash. If neither was soon forthcoming, it would have to disband. *So, wait!*

Bonnivet had other views, and the ear of the King.

"We French," said the High Admiral, "have not been

wont to make war by means of military artifice, but handsomely and openly, especially when we have at our head a valiant King." Jolting cavalry charges, not siege tactics, were the familiar Bonnivet solution.

He reminded Francis of Melegnano, where "our King here present" had performed so magnificently.

The King, whose luck had been somewhat uneven in the ten years between, was acutely aware of the need for another sweeping victory. Back in 1515, Charles V had not appeared on the European scene. Now he and Francis were locked in a struggle in which the whole continent was at stake.

Francis made his characteristic decision: pitched battle, not watchful waiting. If it were offered, he would accept the challenge of open combat, openly arrived at.

It was now a question of who would throw down the gauntlet.

At their own council of war on February 23, Bourbon and Pescara argued strongly for taking the offensive. Word had come through from de Leyva that he could not hold out for more than a day or two, and this was a powerful argument for swift action. The council voted to attack the next day, and sent a message to de Leyva to be ready to make a sortie at a given signal. Two cannon shots fired in rapid succession from a certain redoubt would be the signal.

Pescara had some vigorous words for his own lean Spaniards. "I cannot feed you, my boys," he said, "but before you lies the camp where there is bread in plenty, meat and wine . . . If you are set on having anything to eat tomorrow, march we down on the French camp."

The action began that same midnight. Hundreds of

Pescara's engineers attacked the splendid walls of Monte-bello with pike and shovel and pick. The night was so dark, with no moon showing, that the men wore white shirts over their armor or big white patches on their doublets so that they could tell friend from foe. A dense ground fog further reduced what little visibility there was.

For four hours, the men worked noisily, so that the French had fair warning of what was going on. By early morning, 300 feet of wall had been cleared. Francis trained his fine artillery on the breach and waited.

It was not yet clear whether a full-dress battle was what the Imperial commanders intended, or simply an attempt to relieve Pavia by pushing a task force through Montebello to the city gates.

Troops began to pour through the breach, and it was soon apparent that a good part of the Imperial army was involved. Galiot de Genouillac's impeccable artillery went into swift action, mowing down the assailants by the hundreds at very close range.

"You could see nothing," said one witness, "but heads and arms and pieces of armor flying about."

Now Francis unleashed a spirited attack on the enemy advance guard, killing the leader with his own lance. The headlong charge carried him and his chosen knights straight through the relieving force, which gave ground on all sides. Francis reined in at last to rest the horses.

The battle seemed to be won. In his joy he turned to the Marshal de Foix, who had ridden beside him.

"Now I really can call myself Duke of Milan!" he said.

In his magnificent silver coat of mail, studded with the

golden lilies of France, with his great plumed helmet and flashing sword, he did indeed look like the embodiment of victory. But the truth was that such a charge, with no supporting infantry to make firm the wedge that was driven, was already a tactic of the past. The enemy closed in again like waters in the wake of a swift vessel.

The raid-in-force was full battle now, or rather a series of isolated battles, whose sum would mean victory or defeat.

Suddenly everything seemed to be going wrong for the French. In the confusion, some of Francis's foot soldiers marched straight in front of Galiot de Genouillac's artillery, masking his line of fire. The ground was so sodden that the guns could not be shifted. At a crucial moment, they were forced to remain silent.

Now Pescara's 1,500 riflemen went smartly into action against the French left flank. Their new shoot-retire-reload tactic worked perfectly, and the flank gave ground before the precise and deadly fire. At the same time Bourbon's German soldiers of fortune were locked in a brutal hand-to-hand, pike-to-pike struggle with the renowned Swiss, led by Fleuranges. Surprisingly, despite the heroism of the Young Adventurer, it was the Swiss who broke and ran.

By now it was eight o'clock in the morning.

The Imperial bugles were sounding fresh orders through the fog. The French guns were still sullenly silent. Suddenly two cannon shots in rapid succession roared out from the Imperial camp. Right on cue, de Leyva came swarming out of the main gate of Pavia with a picked regiment of riflemen and dismounted cavalry, causing a tumult in the French rear.

The Battle of Pavia, by a Flemish follower of Patenier

Alençon, hearing that the left flank had been turned, fearing the day was lost, now did the unforgivable. In fair order he and some 10,000 troops withdrew from the field. Even worse, he destroyed the boat bridge over the Ticino after only 4,000 had crossed. Some 6,000 Swiss mercenaries were left to drown in the swift waters as retreat turned into panic.

All this reached Francis by tremor and rumor across miles of fog and smoke, and the roar of battle.

"My God," he yelled, "what is the matter? What is happening?"

A kind of madness comes over the King as the tide of battle goes against him. With fifty of his household cavalry he hurls himself into the enemy ranks, as if to turn the tide and churn his way to freedom by sheer momentum and desperate courage.

First he orders his bugler to sound a high note on his silver trumpet, the call for help of the King in mortal danger. But the note is too high or too late, for no help comes.

The bravest of the brave are with him as he attacks. The enemy discharge their arquebuses at point-blank range, and no armor can withstand this new kind of concentrated fire. First the Spanish riflemen aim for the horse at some vulnerable point. When the horse falls, the knight is thrown sprawling in his heavy armor. Only a man of great strength can even struggle to his feet, let alone defend himself. The foot soldiers then kill at leisure by musket and dagger.

In this way La Palice falls, a few yards from his King.

A Spanish soldier thrusts the barrel of his arquebus through a chink in his armor and blows the fine old warrior to glory.

"I cannot outlive this day," cries Bonnivet, chief architect of the day and its shambles. He opens his visor and spurs into the foe. Three pikes pierce his armor, and still he lays about him with his blade. Finally, losing consciousness, he falls on his horse's neck, and the horse bears his body from the field.

The Bastard of Savoy strangles inside his own helmet. Saint-Sevrin, the Master of the Royal Horse, is the victim of a close volley. His stiff armor holds him in the saddle. Stone dead, he gallops about the field for what seems an endless time. Finally, riddled by a hundred shots, he topples from his horse.

The Comte de Saint-Pol is killed near Francis, and then the Marshal de Foix goes down. La Trémoille, veteran of a score of battles, dies as he would wish, with the clang of steel around and above him.

The chronicles of the time speak of these men as having been "crowned by death," and this seems right and true. They had all lived by the sword and for the sword, and to die defending one's king is no mean thing.

Francis himself almost escapes. He puts his horse at a stone wall, with freedom on the far side. Just as the horse gathers his feet for the leap, a shot in the head fells him.

Using his great strength, Francis steps clear as the horse goes down. He tries to cut a path with his sweeping sword. Two Spaniards fall, but half a dozen more are on him like

*Bust of Francis I in armor, eighteenth-century bronze
after a sixteenth-century original*

jackals—tearing at his rich armor, wounding him in cheek and sword-arm and knee.

Inside his helmet, Francis drinks his own blood and sweat —and fights on as the Spaniards close for the kill. No mercy here for man or monarch!

At the exact critical moment, Lannoy comes spurring up, laying about him with the flat of his sword. He dismounts at Francis's side, screens him with his own body.

"Seigneur Viceroy, I surrender to you," Francis gasps.

"Sire, do not doubt it, your life will be safe," says Lannoy, accepting the great sword.

The Viceroy clears a path through his snarling, loot-crazed soldiers, and at last the captive King reaches safety.

Francis's wounds were slight. He asked not to be taken into Pavia as a spectacle for all to gaze at. His captors honored the request, and he was escorted to a small fortress called Pizzighettone. There he was placed in a tower room with barred windows looking out on the endless plain.

From Pizzighettone he wrote his mother the celebrated letter which begins: "Madame, to let you know the full extent of my misfortune, nothing is left to me except my honor and my life, which is safe."

As time passed, this sentence would go into legend, into history in simplified form: "All is lost save honor."

Chapter 18

THE TOWER
IN THE PLAIN

The battle of Pavia was for the French a mitigated disaster. Over 10,000 of her soldiers were killed—almost ten times the Imperial losses. All Genouillac's splendid guns fell into enemy hands, along with the great gunner himself. Among the other prisoners of war held for ransom were the King of Navarre, the Prince of Talmont, the Duke of Montmorency, Fleuranges, and Clément Marot the poet. The loot, in rich armor, weapons, and supplies, was fabulous.

On the other hand, the spirit of the French people proved remarkably strong in adversity. When Louise of Savoy heard the terrible news, she said, "The King is a prisoner but France lives." And she moved vigorously to make sure that the nation would continue to do so.

Marshal Lautrec, who had survived the battle and escaped, served as her principal lieutenant. With his seasoned help she saw to it that the remnants of the army which straggled back from Italy were paid and put to work. Better still, she arranged for Andrea Doria and the Genoese fleet to transport the Duke of Albany and his 10,000 soldiers home from Italy—unscathed—to help defend the realm.

In effect, the French closed ranks, and their morale in defeat remained high. One source of pride was Francis himself. Even if he had turned out to be a foolish general, he had been brave in battle. In Fleuranges's diary there is a typical tribute: "As long as he had men with him, he fought . . . Finally, when all others had gone away, he had his horse killed under him, and went on defending himself sword in hand as bravely as prince ever did."

So the mantle of hero settled over Francis's broad shoulders. Moreover, the gallant death of so many of his noblemen showed the French that their leaders still possessed that most ancient and epic of virtues: the ability to die for one's country.

There is a jingle of the time that tells us a lot. It concerns the fate of that grand old soldier, Marshal La Palice, symbol of all the other exemplary deaths at Pavia. The poem starts like this:

> *Monsieur de La Palice is dead*
> *In Pavia's mortal strife;*
> *Fifteen minutes before his death*
> *He was still very much in life.*

There are many more verses, just as simple and obvious. The little song, with its palpable truth about French valor at Pavia, has gone into folklore. French schoolboys still sing it today, and the French phrase for a truism is a *verité de La Palice.*

On the Duke of Alençon, the one coward of the terrible and glorious day of battle, Louise of Savoy unleashed all

her disciplined fury. Her scorn, and that of his fellow coun-
trymen, was too much for him. Two months after he stumbled back across the Alps, poor dull craven Alençon died
of pleurisy and remorse, leaving Marguerite of Angoulême a
widow something less than bereft.

France did survive. Under the high, slow-moving clouds of
her blue-domed sky, the earth turned and the seasons spun.
Her peasants went on plowing, and her towns throve. After
a while, with the free-spending Francis still in captivity,
Louise of Savoy's austere budget began to show a modest
profit.

Francis had expected to be treated according to the laws
of chivalry, meaning a large ransom and a quick release.
The courtesy with which Lannoy and Pescara and the em-
barrassing Bourbon treated him seemed at first to justify
this hope.

Shortly after the battle, his captors sent for the King's
royal robes and Court dress, wanting him to appear the
prize of prizes that he was. The retreating French handed
them over. So Francis soon looked a bird of fine plumage
again. By contrast, Pescara, who was often in attendance,
wore sober black, making the Spanish marshal seem more
like a captive than the French King did.

"How do you think," Francis asked Pescara one day,
"that the Emperor will behave to me?"

"I believe," Pescara answered, "that I can answer for the
Emperor's moderation. I am sure he will make a generous
use of his victory."

How little he knew his Flemish master!

Already, at twenty-five, Charles was old, with a kind of melancholy that he only shed at table. He ate and drank so avidly that gout set in early. His legs were too short for his body. His beard was carefully trimmed in an attempt to conceal the underslung jaw. But it was the jaw—so powerful that it was almost a deformity—that gave the clue: this merchant among kings, on whose dominions the sun never set, this joyless bourgeois monarch with his motto of "More Beyond," was and would always be a formidable enemy of the more knightly, more open-hearted Francis. Secret, cold, relentless, he was the sort of man who would drain the cup of victory to the dregs.

At the time of Francis's imprisonment the Imperial fortress of Pizzighettone was strong indeed, with four towers, flanking walls, and a great central keep. Today only one tower remains, doing double duty as a water tower. It happens to be the tower where Francis was held. You can still see the small barred window out of which he gazed so long and longingly at the wide Lombard plain. The iron bars that he gripped in the timeless way of all prisoners are still in place.

Francis spent several months at Pizzighettone. He was closely guarded but not badly treated. On good days he exercised in the castle courtyard, and he was allowed some visitors. With money loaned by Lannoy, he bought books, a pug dog, two finches. But fifty times a day, and more often at night, a guard would open the heavy door to make

Museo del Prado

Charles V, detail of a painting by Titian

sure that he had not miraculously flown. So he was never allowed to forget his misery for long.

In the outside world, there was a good deal of reappraisal, some agonizing, some in the name of plain common sense. Even though he fawned all over Francis when he saw him, Bourbon was bellowing for the dismemberment of France. In his vengeful plans, one of the key invaders was, as always, Henry VIII. When the English King first heard the news of Francis's defeat, he wept for joy. But soon he took a longer second look. It did not really suit him to have his Hapsburg nephew grow too strong. So the endless balancing act began again. Urged on by Wolsey (who was still brooding over his lost Papacy), Henry began to explore the possibility of a treaty of peace and friendship with Louise the Regent.

Italy too was veering away from the Emperor. In the duchy of Milan, Charles's poorly paid soldiers were living brutally off the land and making themselves hated for doing so. Florentine Pope Clement wrote to Francis of his fears that the whole peninsula would be overrun by Charles. Venice, the great Republic of the Sea, looked to her landward moorings.

How Charles would treat his famous prisoner was of concern to all. At last, on March 28, 1525, over a month after Pavia, the Emperor sent his harsh terms to Pizzighettone.

To be free again, Francis would have to:

—Give up, forever, all attempts to conquer Italy.

—Surrender the great duchy of Burgundy, which Charles

claimed through his great-grandfather, Charles the Bold (its last duke).

—Reinstate Bourbon in all his lands and give him Provence and Dauphiny as well.

—Pay a huge ransom.

—Forfeit the countships of Flanders and Artois.

—Hand over his two oldest sons as hostages, until all the terms were fulfilled.

Burgundy was the bone of contention here, for it had fallen to the French crown by default many years before. As well as being a strong defensive frontier, it had become an integral part of the kingdom. But many of the other terms were almost equally shocking to Francis.

The Viceroy of Naples, who had grown to like and admire the King, was puzzled and surprised too.

Lannoy and Francis had many long talks about what to do. Francis dug in his heels about giving up Burgundy. On other terms he was less adamant, and quite realistic about creating what he saw was an independent kingdom for Bourbon.

"I agree," he said, "but may I never set eyes on him again!"

Both Lannoy and Francis felt that it was vitally important for Francis to meet his "cousin" the Emperor face to face. Such a confrontation, they believed, or perhaps just hoped, would make the young-old Charles relent, and relax some of the harsher terms.

Bringing this about would not be easy, as they knew well. Pescara and Bourbon, each for his own reasons, wanted to keep the King in Italy. And it was out of character for the Emperor to journey there to see his prisoner.

Viceroy and captive King worked out a secret plot which would take even the Emperor by surprise.

First, Lannoy convinced Pescara and Bourbon that their royal prisoner would be safer in the great citadel of Naples.

They agreed.

On May 18, Francis, in the close company of several thousand Imperial troops, left his tower in the plain. Six days later he was at Genoa, where sixteen ships and a sea-going bodyguard of 2,000 arquebusiers waited to shepherd him south.

Now came part two, the tricky part: the convoy sailed for Naples all right, but either bad weather or good planning caused it to put in at Portofino, a few miles down the Ligurian coast.

Andrea Doria and the Duke of Montmorency materialized out of the blue Mediterranean to blockade the flotilla there. Together they had twenty-five ships and 4,000 men. Montmorency, who had been freed by the Spaniards the month before in exchange for a ranking Imperial officer, had been appointed by Louise of Savoy her seagoing commander. The first thing he did was to join forces with the most celebrated seaman of the time.

What happened next stemmed from the new friendship of Lannoy and Francis, and from the chivalrous nature of each. Both were still convinced that a meeting with Charles was the answer to everything.

So the two fleets merged amicably. Then a mixed convoy

of twenty-five galleys was formed to escort Francis to Spain instead of Naples.

Lannoy informed no one, not even his master Charles V, of the change of plan.

Neither King nor Viceroy could have guessed what heart-break lay ahead. How, in their knightly innocence, could they have known that Charles was inflexible in his determination—that Francis must be made to pay for both his folly and his fame?

Chapter 19

THE TOWER
IN THE TOWN

The flotilla arrived at Barcelona on June 19, 1525. There, in the chief city of Catalonia, Francis received a thundering welcome. Something about the captive King appealed to the Catalans, whose sense of honor and high-minded code of conduct were legendary. They liked the way he carried himself in defeat and they liked the fact that, unlike their own hideaway Emperor, he had fought magnificently and to the bitter end.

When Francis went to mass in the cathedral, they cheered him through the streets. There was a huge ball in his honor, as well as bullfights and receptions. Once again he breathed air that was almost free, and drank in adulation. Down the coast at Valencia, it was the same royal welcome all over again.

Bourbon and Pescara were of course furious, the former reportedly turning black with rage at the news. But there was not very much that they could do. Bourbon wanted to come to Spain to air his grievances. At one point, Charles V went so far as to ask one of his grandees if he would entertain the Constable.

"I can refuse Your Majesty nothing," the grandee replied, "but as soon as the traitor is out of my house, I will fire it with my own hand; no man of honor could live in it any more."

Brooding away at Valladolid in the arid north, Charles was furious too. It did not suit his plans at all to have his Spanish subjects greet his prisoner like a conquering hero. He summoned Lannoy, preparing to grill him on the coals of his burning anger.

But something quite extraordinary was happening to Charles in Spain. For three years he had been studying his people there, and learning from them. Shrewd Flemish Lowlander that he was, he liked what he saw. Spanish pride and the rigid Spanish code of conduct suited his nature very well indeed.

It was true that Lannoy had gone beyond his instructions in bringing Francis to Spain. But he had shared in a great Imperial victory just before. There was no real reason to diminish him—and one's own dignity as Holy Roman Emperor—by giving in to rage.

Charles received Lannoy with his glossy new Spanish manners beautifully in place. Lannoy, however, got the point quickly enough: *lock the bird up again before it is too late*. The town of Madrid was to be the new cage, and the sooner the better. Charles told Lannoy dryly that he himself had no great wish to meet his captive. Perhaps he would do so, in his own Imperial good time. Or perhaps never.

The tower in the town was a much higher, grimmer place than the tower in the plain had been. Francis's narrow room a hundred feet above the ground had only one door. There was a little alcove for an altar, some chairs and tables, two chests, and a bed not much bigger than a camp cot. From the double-barred window Francis looked out on a sadder scene than the green Lombard plain: the hill town of Madrid straggled unevenly, with a few mangy, black-stone palaces showing. The Manzanares River in summer was just a trickle across the sun-baked soil. Between Francis and freedom were many strong walls and wide moats.

All this was a bitter disappointment to the King. He had arrived in Madrid on August 17, feted and cheered almost to the city gates. He was in no mood for a narrow cell and the clang of armed men at all hours on the stone stair outside.

Two battalions were assigned to guard him, with one of them always on duty. They changed the guard noisily in the big vaulted hall on the ground floor of the tower. One of the officers was stationed in Francis's room at all times.

Shortly after Pavia, Francis had written Charles a letter which showed that he was fully aware of the situation he was in. "I have no other comfort in my plight but reliance on your goodness," he wrote. If Charles did show "honorable pity," Francis went on, "you may be sure of obtaining a benefit instead of a useless prisoner and of making a King of France your slave forever."

Now, as the weeks passed, and no response came from the Emperor, Francis's spirits began to fail. He pined. Since he himself would never give up Burgundy, and Charles it seemed would lay claim to the duchy forever, everything was hopeless. It would be far better to abdicate, or to die.

Suddenly Francis was very ill. Torpid, semi-conscious, he lay on his narrow cot, with his face to the wall and a burning fever. He had an abscess in his nose, a poison through his whole body, and a kind of poison in his soul as well.

Charles at last became concerned. If Francis died, he would have lost hostage and trump card, and this he could not afford.

On September 18, with Lannoy and one torchbearer in attendance, he visited the royal cell.

This first meeting of the two great rivals had its own drama. It was nine at night and Francis was sleeping fitfully. Charles went and stood quietly by the bed. At last the King opened his eyes and saw the Emperor's long, pale, unmistakable face by the flickering torchlight.

He struggled to his feet and the two men embraced.

"Sire," Francis said in a weak voice, "has Your Majesty come to see your prisoner die?"

"Not my prisoner," Charles protested. "My brother and my friend. I desire nothing more than your health. Think only of that. All the rest will come as you wish it."

"It must be as you command," Francis's sad voice replied. "But, Sire, I beg you, let there be no intermediary between us."

Then he fell back exhausted on the bed.

The next morning he was worse. Fully alarmed now, Charles visited him again. Faintly, Francis begged Charles to take care of his children after he was gone. As he left the cell, Charles met a weeping woman coming up the circular stair. She was dressed in simple black and wore the white veil of a royal widow. He knew her at once. For, some weeks before, when Francis began his decline, he had given permission for her to come.

It was Marguerite of Angoulême.

She and the Emperor embraced and Charles said he knew that she had come in time. She murmured between sobs that she hoped so.

By ship from Aigues-Mortes to Barcelona, then by litter during nine jolting days, she had made all possible speed. Yet the hours seemed endless, and to make them pass more quickly she had written some verses that still brim with emotion. They began:

> *For the bliss that awaits me, so strong*
> *Is my yearning that yearning is pain;*
> *One hour a hundred years long;*
> *My litter, it bears me in vain—*

Now Marguerite stood by the bedside. But this time Francis did not recognize his visitor. He lay in deep coma, and the quiet that filled the room was the terrible stillness that contains the acceptance of death.

With all the weapons of sisterly love and deep religious faith, Marguerite went into action. For three days she never left Francis's side. She had mass said at the little altar in the alcove, and constant prayers by her own matrons and Francis's small household staff.

On the third day, while the Archbishop of Embrun was intoning the mass, the King opened his eyes.

"It is my God who will cure me body and soul," he said, indicating his wish to share in the Communion. The Archbishop divided a wafer, giving half to Marguerite and half to the King.

Francis managed to swallow his half, and suddenly he seemed a little better.

It was the turning point. The abscess broke soon after, and the fever fell. He began to eat and drink and sleep in a normal way.

By October, thanks to his splendid vitality and renewed will to live, he was himself again.

Marguerite turned to the urgent matter of his freedom. She went to the ancient city of Toledo, where Charles was staying. At the gate of the Alcazar he greeted her gravely and himself escorted her from her carriage. They were alone for two hours, the young bachelor Emperor and the brilliant, enchanting widow. But all her brilliance and enchantment were like water breaking on stone.

Even her most ingenious plan failed. She suggested that Charles be given Burgundy as he demanded, then that Francis marry Charles's sister Eleanor (who, like all Spain, was a little in love with him already). Then, let Eleanor's dowry be Burgundy!

"No," said Charles with his stubborn Lowland logic. "In that way, you give it to me and I have to give it back. What I want is to get it and keep it."

He reminded her that Eleanor was promised to Bourbon. Marguerite nodded, but sensed that she had planted a

Eleanor of Austria, portrait by van Cleve

thought there. After all, Bourbon was only a duke and Francis was King. And for looks and gallantry and noble bearing there really was no comparison!

For the moment she had failed and she knew it. She went back to Francis with new advice. Sign whatever they ask. Give up Burgundy. Forget Italy forever. Let your sons be hostages if they must. Anything to be free! Before you sign, explain in private to your retainers that you are acting as a prisoner under duress. Then afterwards, when you really are free, repudiate everything.

The third member of the famous trinity was writing along the same lines. Louise hammered away at Francis, echoing Marguerite's logic and her persuasive eloquence, and at the same time she sent a skilled team of negotiators to hammer out the exact terms of a treaty. *Just sign!*

The hitch was that Francis really did live by a knightly code—which he called his *foi de gentilhomme*. He lived by and for this faith of a gentleman, and to ask him to renounce it was asking a very great deal.

At this point, Charles made one concession. As Marguerite had guessed, he broke his longtime promise that Bourbon would marry Eleanor. How he did this was simple enough: he asked Eleanor to take her choice. Without hesitation, Eleanor said she preferred the comely King to the dark, scowling duke.

Pressed hard by the two women he never could resist for long, faced by one concession at last on the part of the Emperor, Francis gave in. He agreed to sign anything and everything, and to swear the most solemn oath that he would live up to the terms of the treaty.

The final document was brought to him on January 14, 1526. The day before, he had called his own small staff together in secret. He told them that he rejected in advance what he was about to do, and that he had only been forced to agree to the treaty because of the hardship of his long imprisonment.

Then, with an almost terrifying zest, he plunged into the ceremonies. Even if he was betraying his code of honor—his faith of a gentleman that was almost his religion—he seemed to say: *let me at least do so in style.*

Using the altar in the little alcove, a mass was celebrated to sanctify the signatures. Then Francis signed, first as King and again as true knight. Lannoy the Viceroy represented the Emperor, along with two other witnesses. Three Frenchmen—the Archbishop of Embrun, Jean de Selve, and Chabot de Brion—testified for Francis's good intent.

After signing, the King placed his hand in Lannoy's and spoke in a clear, firm voice: "I, Francis the First, King of France and nobleman, pledge my faith to the Emperor Charles that if within six weeks after the Emperor has set me free in my own realm of France, I have not restored to him the duchy of Burgundy . . . I will return to the Emperor's power, to remain in prison wherever it shall please the said Emperor to order me, until the contents of the said treaty shall be utterly fulfilled."

So he was free to go at last. But something of his true self died within him even as he spoke.

Chapter 20

THE CROSSROADS
AND THE RIVER

Francis would not really be free until he reached France again. There was still a certain amount of rather solemn Spanish ritual before he was able to do so. First came another ceremony in the small room in the tower, marking Francis's formal engagement to Eleanor. This time, Lannoy the ever present stood in for the Emperor's sister and made the responses which entitled Francis to call her his Queen from that moment onward.

On February 16, Francis and the Emperor met at the gates of Madrid and rode together into the country for a three-day visit to Eleanor. The visit went very well. Since Eleanor was young and vivacious, if not exactly beautiful, she made an excellent impression. When she fell to her knees and tried to kiss Francis's hand, he lifted her up.

"It is not the hand I owe you but the lips," he said in his gallant way, and sealed their engagement with a hearty kiss.

When it came to parting, Francis and Charles were more like new brothers-in-law than old enemies. The Emperor was on his way west to Portugal for his own marriage to

Queen Isabella. Francis was heading north, via Madrid, to the French frontier.

They rode together awhile, at some distance from their escorts. When they neared the crossroads, Charles had his moment of misgiving.

"My brother," he said, "do you remember what you have agreed with me to do?"

"I remember so well that I could repeat the articles by heart."

"Since you know them so well, tell me if you intend to fulfill them, or if you find some difficulty there? For in such case we would find that we would be enemies again."

"I intend to accomplish the treaty in full and I know that no one in my kingdom will oppose this. If you see that I act differently, I wish and consent that you consider me evil and cowardly."

"I want you to say the same for me, if I do not give you back your freedom. Above all, I ask you one thing, and that is not to fail me in the matter of my sister, now your wife, for that would be an injury that I would deeply resent and would have to avenge."

Their escorts closed around them as they reined in under the signposts pointing to Madrid and to Torreon in the west. There the velvet-and-iron Emperor and the now-devious King embraced.

"God keep you, my brother!"

"My brother, God keep you!"

They wheeled and turned and went their separate ways.

The Bidassoa River, which in its lower reaches divides France and Spain, rises in the Pyrenees and empties into the Bay of Biscay. A few miles upriver from the bay and at its exact middle—on the thread of the river—a pontoon with a platform on it had been moored, the day before Francis was to cross into freedom.

On the day itself—March 17, 1526—at seven in the morning, when the tide was full, two boats set out simultaneously from the two banks of the river. Each had an equal number of oarsmen, and they arrived at the floating platform at the same instant.

Francis and Lannoy the Viceroy were in the craft which moved out from the Spanish shore. The Dauphin Francis and his younger brother Henry, Duke of Orléans, were in the one from the French side of the river. Their escorting officer was Marshal Lautrec.

Both boys were lively and alert. They had been told that they were to see their father and then go on to Spain, but not much more. The word "hostage" may have been mentioned, but certainly not the word "prisoner." Their ages were ten and eight. They were excited, and they also knew that something was terribly wrong.

The exchange was quickly done. Almost speechless, Francis clasped one son and then the other in his strong arms. A chronicle of the day describes the scene like this:

The good King, when he saw his children, had pity for them at the thought that they were going into prison so young, and could find no words but to tell them to take care of themselves, to eat plenty and that soon he would send to fetch them . . . So the two young princes passed into Spain, and the King into his most blessed kingdom of France.

When his boat neared the French bank, he leaped into shallow water and waded ashore. Nearly a thousand noblemen, archers, and Swiss guardsmen were there to greet him.

A joy as great as the sorrow of a few minutes before seized him.

"Now I am King! I am King again!" he cried.

Running up the shore, he threw himself upon the fine Turkish horse that a groom was holding for him. Then, to the cheers of his friends and henchmen, he galloped into France, into freedom at last.

BOOK III

The True Glory

This Prince seemed unto me beside
the handsomeness of his person and bewtie of visage,
to have in his countenance a great majestie,
accompanied with a certain lovely courtesie . . .
Among other things it was told me that
he highly loved and esteemed letters.

GIULIO DE' MEDICI

Chapter 21

A STATELY PLEASURE DOME DECREED

Francis had been hurt in his chivalry. The physical wounds which he had suffered at Pavia—a torn ear lobe, gashes in sword-arm and legs—had healed quickly enough. To a man of his sanguine nature, the loneliness and misery of the two towers soon receded into the past. But he had given his word as a gentleman to do certain things which he had no intention of doing. So now, free again, he began to suffer an illness of the spirit—the French might call it a *crise de foi*—which lasted in some degree for the remaining twenty years of his life and rule.

He was thirty-two. He had been in prison for over a year, and away from France for a year and a half. He would never again seek gold and glory in the Italian plains, never again lead men in battle.

He did gather up the reins of power again, so firmly that there was no question, ever, who was master. *"Car tel est notre plaisir"* was a phrase that he used more and more often—"for such is our wish," with no need to justify or explain.

At the same time, having been wounded in spirit by defeat and imprisonment, he was quite content to relinquish many of the cares of government to his mother and to Duprat, the ever-present Chancellor. Not that Francis brooded. He simply turned more and more of his time and interest to the fields where his real excellence lay: to art and letters, architecture and sculpture. As patron, collector, and critic, he now put his exalted rank and excellent taste to splendid and spectacular use.

First of all came pleasures long denied. At Bayonne, after his headlong ride up the coast, he found waiting the three people he cared for most in the world: Louise and Marguerite and Anne de Heilly. So there was love of several kinds, and also the joys of the hunt and the table, and many fetes. Into all these he plunged with gusto.

In prison he had written some sparse, sad verses to help pass the hours. With Clément Marot back in his household to instruct and praise, his poetry grew graceful again. Here is the opening of his tribute to the women he loved:

> *D'en aimer trois ce m'est force et contrainte*
> (To love three is my necessity and my constraint)

Even before Pavia, Francis had started to build a great new palace called Chambord in the sandy, scrub-oak-and-pine country south of the Loire. Now he plunged into its construction with fresh zeal, spending many hours on the scaffolding, leading 1,800 workers in their assault on stone and gravity and tradition.

He had several scale models built to show what the pile would look like when it was done. These he pored over like a general with his maps, moving towers and stairs and galleries the way he had once moved troops.

Some say that the original design was Leonardo da Vinci's. Certainly, King and artist talked a great deal about the creation of a fabulous castle during da Vinci's three years at Amboise. And Chambord's turrets and pinnacles bear a striking resemblance to the sketches in Leonardo's notebooks.

One of the marvels of Chambord is the double-spiral staircase at its center, so designed that someone going up the stair need never meet the person coming down. Its beauty and ingenuity are very Leonardo-like—so this too is cited as evidence of his hand.

Chambord was intended to be a hunting lodge, but it is to all other hunting lodges what the Taj Mahal is to all other tombs. There are 445 rooms, 61 staircases (in addition to the great spiral one at its heart), a chimney for every day in the year. The wall around its fields and forests is twenty miles long and took twelve years to build.

Chambord still rises, as white and mysterious as ever, from its dim countryside. Long before you see it, you feel its presence and its spell. The spoke-like alleys through the sparse forest obviously lead *somewhere*. The mild, carefully tilled fields are in subservience to *something*.

From afar, when it does gleam into sight, it has the bulk and look of a medieval castle, with round drum-towers at the corners and a great central *donjon* or keep. But as you draw nearer it becomes clear that there are no battlements to fire arrows from, or pour down boiling lead. The eight many-windowed towers serve no defensive function, and the

courtyards are galleried for fetes and masked balls, not ultimate onslaughts.

Just as marvelous as the staircase, and more miraculous,
are the roofs of Chambord. While the wings and towers
themselves have an early-Renaissance purity, what crowns
them is like the skyline of some fabled city. There is an
ordered confusion of campanile and buttress, dome and
pinnacle, that pays exuberant tribute to the great central
lantern tower. Topped by a stone *fleur de lis* some 150 feet
from the courtyard below, the tower itself is like the last,
triumphant trumpet peal in this cadenza in stone.

Construction went on from 1524 to the end of Francis's
reign, and after. It never was quite finished, never fully
furnished. Somewhere along the line Francis lost interest.
He spent only a month or two there in all, after the main
work was done. Nor has much happened since. Gaston of
Orléans and his daughter, the Great Mademoiselle, once
played tag on the spiral staircase; Louis XIV and his vast
retinue came to hunt there from time to time. Today, off
season, when the tourists are not trooping through its vast-
ness, Chambord seems to brood, a little sadly, over its empty
fate and its lack of history.

Historian Francis Hackett has summed up Chambord in
a sentence. He said that it "had no excuse except that it
really represented the scale of indulgence at which Francis
aimed."

The scale of indulgence! Francis would use the scale to
take the measure of other already existing palaces—Blois
and Fontainebleau and the Louvre—and to create new

Chambord

beauty in them that far transcends the whited sepulchre of Chambord.

And yet . . . and yet . . . Chambord is somehow more typical of its time. For it seems to be one answer to that craving for the marvelous which was in the blood and bone of Renaissance man.

Chapter 22

THE PENDULUM
SWINGS

Always there, even among his prodigal pleasures, was the problem of repudiating the Treaty of Madrid. Sooner or later something had to be done, for Charles V and Lannoy were pressing Francis hard to translate its terms into action.

While Francis suffered from having made false promises, he had no intention of keeping them. What he wanted was to put together as good a case as possible for repudiation.

First, he called a group of leading Burgundian nobles and citizens to Cognac. They willingly testified that they wished the duchy to remain French.

Then, in December of 1527, Francis went to Paris and spoke to a packed Parlement. With eloquence, even grandeur, he reviewed his reign, not trying in any way to hide his failures.

"If my subjects have suffered," he said, "I have suffered with them." He offered to return to a Spanish prison if such was the will of the Parlement, but he reminded his listeners that he had been under great pressure when he had given his word to all the harsh terms of the treaty. After four days' discussion, the Parlement decreed that he was under no obligation to live up to it. They pointed out that Burgundy was not really his to give away in any case, and they voted him two million crowns to ransom his sons.

When he heard the news, Charles V allowed himself to go into cold rage. He told the French ambassador in Madrid that his master had acted like a "dastard and a scoundrel in not keeping his word."

In actual fact, the Emperor was no longer in a position to do much about it, for the pendulum of power was swinging away from him in Francis's favor.

Across the Channel, Henry VIII was taking the first steps to divorce Catherine of Aragon and marry Anne Boleyn. This could not fail to alienate her nephew the Emperor and to reduce the prospects of any real Spanish–English alliance.

In Germany, Martin Luther's driving wish to reform the Church had become open revolt from it, threatening to shake the foundations of Catholicism and of the Holy Roman Empire.

Equally dangerous to Charles's hope of achieving a workable Empire was the rise of Suleiman the Turk, later known as the Magnificent. He was pressing hard on Charles's eastern frontiers. Soon he would conquer Hungary and lay siege to Vienna itself.

Italy was in its usual state of chaos. Alarmed at the increasing power of the Emperor there, Pope Clement VII, the eternal waverer, for once took sides. He organized a new Holy League against Charles, persuading Milan and Venice to join it. France and England, less openly, signed on as well.

It was clear that the Emperor had to take decisive action, or the victory at Pavia would come to nothing.

Charles was short of top lieutenants. Pescara had died, and he needed Lannoy by his side. So he had no choice but to give Bourbon the overall command in Italy. The Constable was as usual out of money and out of temper. Francis's repudiation of the treaty meant that he had lost any chance of regaining his ancestral lands. He managed to recruit some 15,000 greedy German mercenaries, mostly Lutherans who were delighted to serve against the Pope and the Holy League. His command also included a Spanish army of sorts.

Since the Pope was the prime mover in challenging the Emperor's control, Rome was the focal point of the campaign. On March 5, 1527, Bourbon's motley army was in sight of the Eternal City. The next day he led the assault on its moldering walls.

Characteristically, he wore a silver jacket over his armor, making him a marked man to friend and foe alike. Just as he started up one of the scaling ladders, an arquebus shot from along the walls tore into his left side. Bourbon fell back into the ditch. Sensing that the wound was mortal, he told his men to cover him with a cloak so that the troops would not lose heart. They did so, and the troops swept past him as he lay dying, surged up the ladders irresistibly, and took the city by storm.

So died Charles de Montpensier, Duke of Bourbon and sometime Constable of France. Whatever else can be said about this great, ill-starred man, the gleaming pride and the courage were his to the bitter end. Even the treason had a kind of grandeur.

With the news of their leader's death, soldiers went wild. No one but the Constable could have held them in check. The killing and looting lasted seven days. While Pope Clement cowered in the castle of Sant' Angelo, cardinals and bishops were butchered, and Roman citizens by the thousands. A million crowns in ransom money was extorted from some of the richer Romans who escaped with their lives.

All Europe was shocked by the sack of Rome, and Charles V pretended to be. "We would rather have been beaten than to have gained such a victory," he said piously. In actual fact, the Emperor was not too unhappy. He was rid of Bourbon, his claims and his fiery arrogance. Pope Clement, who had defied him, was in his power.

Charles V soon managed to restore some measure of order. But he was in no position to take any offensive action against Francis for repudiating the treaty.

He simply contented himself by making the lot of the two little princes harder than ever. The Frenchmen who had accompanied them were withdrawn, so that they never heard their own language spoken. Their only companion was a puppy, and they were moved to a narrower, damper cell in their mountain fastness.

Inevitably, Charles also kept Eleanor in Spain, where she ate her heart out for the will-o'-the-wisp of a husband whom fate had found for her and now had snatched away.

In a medieval gesture, the Emperor challenged Francis to hand-to-hand combat for his sin of repudiation. Francis's answer, written in his own hand, shows how sensitive he had grown on the subject of his honor.

We give you to understand that, if you have intended or do intend to charge us with anything that a gentleman loving his honor ought not to do, we say that you have lied in your throat, and that, as often as you say so, you will lie. Wherefore for the future write us nothing at all; but appoint us the time and place of meeting, and we will bring our sword for you to cross.

There was a great deal of excitement over the challenge, and the coming and going of many heralds. But the whole episode was really a last gasp of the code of chivalry, and the two would-be combatants may well have been just going through the motions.

Francis did seek to exploit Charles's Italian problems by sending Marshal Lautrec into Italy with an army. Ironically, the veteran Lautrec recaptured Pavia with hardly a struggle. Then, moving south toward Naples, he wasted his army in a number of inconclusive battles, caught the plague, and died on August 15, 1528.

Everyone was tired of war, especially the King and the Emperor. A treaty of peace, not a meeting in single, mortal combat, was the obvious answer. Two very sensible and able women were picked to work out the details—Louise of Savoy and Charles's hardheaded aunt, Margaret of Austria.

In the summer of 1529, they met at Cambrai, the small independent state between northern France and the Low Countries. There they worked so calmly and sensibly that the Peace of Cambrai—the Ladies' Peace as it came to be called—satisfied everyone and was quickly signed.

Here were the terms:

—Charles gave up his claim to Burgundy.

—Francis yielded on all his claims to Flemish and Italian territory.

—In return for a ransom of two million crowns, the little princes were set free.

—The marriage of Francis and Eleanor was reconfirmed.

Francis went to Bordeaux to greet his sons and welcome his new wife. For six months there were fetes and galas all over France—royal ones at Cognac and Amboise, Blois and Paris as the Court moved slowly north.

Peace had broken out at last.

$\mathcal{C}$hapter 23

THE STAIN
OF SEMBLANÇAY

Allowing Louise of Savoy to negotiate the Ladies' Peace was a good example of Francis's willingness to relinquish some of his royal powers. His mother was of course almost his second self. During his imprisonment she had once again proved herself a splendid regent. So it was fitting that the much-needed, greatly longed-for peace should be in good part her creation.

Earlier, there had been another episode which showed Louise in a far less appealing light, and which reflected little credit on Francis himself.

This was the Semblançay affair.

Jacques de Beaune, Baron of Semblançay, was a financial wizard. Born in 1454 at Tours, he had ably served three French kings before Francis's time, and managed Anne of Brittany's household as well. He had a pleasant manner which smoothly concealed driving ambition and a matching greed. For eight years, under Francis, he was in effect the master financier, handling the private income of the royal family, deftly juggling private and public funds as required by the King's vast and sudden needs in war and peace.

When taxes could be squeezed no higher, Semblançay could always find the necessary money somewhere, in the shadowy world of moneylenders and Italian bankers at Lyons and elsewhere. If some of the gold stuck to his fingers, who was to be the first to blame him? Francis was lavish in his praises, addressing him as "my father" in tribute to his great age and his skills. Louise gave him the rich barony of Semblançay and the title that went with it.

As he rose in rank and power, Semblançay inevitably made enemies. Chancellor Duprat, who liked to hold all the power there was available in his own plump fingers, was one. Louise became another. That was in 1522, when Semblançay accused her of withholding those 400,000 crowns for her own use—crowns which were meant for Lautrec's troops in Italy.

By the following year, it was obvious that something was very wrong with the muddled, overstrained finances of the realm. A streamlining of the whole immensely complicated tax structure was undertaken, and a new office, Treasurer of the National Savings, created. The post was given to a mortal enemy of Semblançay, and he himself was relieved of all official duties.

The wizard went into retirement. He spent part of his time at his pleasant castles of Beaune and Semblançay, and often stayed in great splendor at his fine townhouse in Tours.

Louise pursued him still. In March 1524, she arranged for a Royal Commission to look into his tangled affairs. His own stock at Court was falling fast, for he now refused to find money for Francis, who needed vast sums for his new

Italian campaign. The King already owed him a million and a half livres, and Semblançay was in no mood to lend any more. The letters beginning *"mon père"* were frequent and urgent now, but the financier was no longer touched by them as he once had been.

During the King's absence and imprisonment, Louise the Regent had other, more pressing problems, but in January 1527, she struck again. Semblançay was arrested without warning, clapped into the Bastille, and promptly put on trial for his life. The charges: falsifying the King's accounts, diverting state money to his own use, selling offices of the crown for private gain, and taking his own cut out of money intended for military supplies and for the royal household. The judges: all Louise's men and Duprat's. Semblançay protested in bitter anger.

The Baron was over eighty, but life and the honors that had come to him were still sweet. He fought like a lion, but the result was foreordained. The verdict, rendered on August 9, 1527, was: *guilty on all counts*. He was stripped of all titles and honors. All his goods and inheritances were confiscated. He himself was condemned to be hanged like a common criminal on the great public gallows of Montfaucon outside Paris.

Semblançay wrote a humble letter to the King: "I implore you to pardon me if I have not served you as well as I possibly could and that it may please you to have pity on my wife and children."

For once, Francis turned a deaf ear. Caught up in his pattern of pleasures—busy, too, with ways and means of repudiating the Treaty of Madrid—he ignored the plea and refused any mitigation of the harsh sentence. In punishing Semblançay, he was of course yielding to Louise, as he almost invariably did. He was also striking at the whole mare's-nest of money—its need and its lack—and serving fair warning to many other money men that the public till was not to be dipped into by private hands.

On the morning of the third day after the sentence was handed down, the gates of the Bastille swung open and a grim troop appeared. Lieutenant Maillart, one of the Provosts of the city, was in charge—a stoop-shouldered man with a furtive, hangdog look about him. There were scores of archers and halberdiers in steel helmets and breastplates. In their midst, mounted on a mule, came Semblançay in a heavy gray robe. His hands were unbound, his dignity unimpaired.

One of the medieval customs that still held was for a state execution to be a kind of public holiday. The streets were lined with spectators. Usually such a crowd would taunt the victim with raucous jeers. Semblançay's great age, his fine white head, and the calmness with which he faced his ordeal, imposed respect. The crowd was subdued, almost silent as he went by.

The cavalcade halted momentarily at the Church of the Filles-Dieu. There, by custom, the condemned man was given bread and wine, and a big wooden cross to hold.

At the hill of Montfaucon, below the high square gallows, there was a terrible three-hour wait in case of a last-minute reprieve. Semblançay must have remembered, in bitter sadness and waning hope, how the King's mercy had come to Saint-Vallier just as the headsman's axe was about to fall.

Toward sunset of the luminous August day, Maillart gave the signal that the moment had come. Almost unaided, Semblançay climbed the tall ladder. He stood quietly looking out over the fair land while the executioner adjusted the noose.

Seconds later, he was swinging in space.

Sometime during the night his corpse was cut down and given decent burial. This was against the specific instructions of Duprat, whose hatred pursued his enemy into death and beyond.

The public, moved by Semblançay's courage, tended to believe his innocence. Some verses by Clément Marot boldly mirrored the people's mood:

> *When Maillart, officer of hell, escorted*
> *To Montfaucon Semblançay, doomed to die,*
> *Which, to your thinking, of the twain supported*
> *The better 'havior? I will make reply:*
> *Maillart was like the man to death proceeding*
> *And Semblançay so stout an ancient looked,*
> *It seemed, forsooth, as if himself were leading*
> *Lieutenant Maillart—to the gallows booked!*

The best that can be said for this sad affair is that it was atypical. A vindictive Louise and a Francis untrue to his basic compassion and fairness of mind both seem very much out of character. It was one of the rare examples of willful cruelty in the life of either.

An anecdote of the day sheds some light. Francis had a habit of calling the beautiful Duchesse d'Uzès *"ma fille."*

One afternoon some of her friends found her in tears and asked why.

"Alas," she said, "the King has just now called me his daughter three or four times over. I have great fear that he will give me the same treatment that he gave M. de Semblançay, whom he so often called his father."

When the King heard the story he laughed, but Louise of Savoy was not amused. She reprimanded the duchess severely, for, as one chronicler put it, "this touched her very closely."

Chapter 24

DA VINCI, CELLINI, AND COMPANY

It was not the least of Francis's virtues that he got along well with genius. Some of the most gifted men of his age enjoyed his company, just as much as he enjoyed theirs. The fact that he met Leonardo da Vinci so early in his career contributed a great deal to this developing skill.

Leonardo had never been an easy man. As far back as 1495, when he was painting *The Last Supper* for Ludovico Sforza, then Duke of Milan, he seemed to be taking an endless time on the great project. The Prior of Santa Maria delle Grazie, site of the mural, complained to the duke about Leonardo's delays, and Sforza asked for an explanation.

"Men of genius are doing most when they work least," the artist told the duke. He went on to say that he had been having trouble visualizing the features of Judas Iscariot. To depict the arch-traitor of all time, the man who betrayed the Creator, was no easy matter!

"But now," said Leonardo, "I am willing to end my search for a model. For lack of a better one, I will use the head of the Prior of Santa Maria." And he did.

Francis first met Leonardo just after the battle of Melegnano. The friendship ripened quickly. The King bought the *Mona Lisa* for 4,000 écus, doubling the number of da Vincis in France. (Louis XII's modest collection had already included the *Madonna of the Rocks*.)

Francis invited Leonardo to France, and the great man, tired of fighting with his Italian patrons, accepted. Shortly afterward, he crossed the Alps by muleback with two of his masterpieces in his saddlebags—the magic *Madonna and Child in the Lap of Saint Anne* and the haunting, disturbing *Saint John the Baptist.*

It is sad that Leonardo never painted his royal friend. The fine eyes of Francis—eyes of a most luminous brown, the straight nose with its quivering nostrils, the general air of aliveness and of tension, would have lent themselves beautifully. But da Vinci, at sixty-four, was old and not well. His right arm had been paralyzed by a recent stroke. Even though he did most of his drawing and painting with his left hand, he was so comfortable at Le Clos-Lucé—with his pleasant little castle and his 700 crowns a year—that the incentive was not very great.

He did design a wonderful gold lion for one of Francis's fetes. The lion spewed lilies from its mouth when the king approached. Some say he created the superb conch-shell staircase at Blois, and cite as evidence the fact that the stair turns to the left.

Mostly Francis and Leonardo talked. Of Chambord and its magnificences-to-come. Of connecting the Seine and the Loire by a series of locks—to navigate and to irrigate as well. Of a palace for Louise at Romorantin with something called a piazza over the river, and of a new sheet of water at Amboise where one could joust from boats. Of philosophy and fortifications, statecraft and the craft of painting, the flight of birds and the possibilities of man's flight.

For three years Francis had the benefit of the most far-ranging mind the world has ever seen. There was nothing exuberant about Leonardo. He could not be called the typical Renaissance man, for his spirit was far too questing, and not confident enough, for that overworked label. In any event, Francis's magnificent vitality and his ability to ask and to listen were the perfect complement.

According to legend, Leonardo died in Francis's arms at Le Clos-Lucé. There are two nineteenth-century paintings to prove it—one good, one terrible. The truth is that on May 3, 1519, the day that da Vinci died, the King was at Saint-Germain for the birth of his second son. He wept when he heard the news.

Leonardo was buried in the chapel of Saint-Hubert at Amboise. During the French Revolution, the tombs there were ransacked and the contents scattered. Later, a broad skull with a magnificent, high cranium was found and re-buried. It is believed to be all that is mortal of the immortal Leonardo.

In the aftermath of the Italian wars, Francis attracted many fine Italian craftsmen to his Court. Il Rosso and Primaticcio were two of the best-known, good, sound painters who were able to plan and administer as well. Andrea del Sarto, a more talented man, came and went. But it was not until 1540 that Francis acquired another true genius.

Benvenuto Cellini, who was born in Florence in the first year of the century, was a brilliant sculptor in bronze and stone, and an even greater worker in precious metals. He was a very different kind of man from Leonardo, a braggart and a brawler. He wrote a diary whose entries read as if they had been jotted down last week, they are so fresh and alive. In the episodes he describes—amatory, warlike, artistic—he always comes out as hero. So you have to remember that everything he wrote must be taken with a grain of salt from one of his own incomparable saltcellars.

Cellini claimed to have fired that shot from the walls of Rome which killed the Duke of Bourbon. He certainly handled gun, sword, and dagger with a skill that almost equaled the way he carved stone and worked metal. Like Leonardo, he quarreled endlessly with his Italian patrons, and welcomed the chance to serve Francis.

There was actually a good deal of bargaining before Cellini agreed to come and settle at the French Court. His price was the price of genius: he insisted on the same 700 crowns a year that Leonardo da Vinci had been given. Francis also loaned him the château de Nesle in Paris to work in, and gave him a title to go with its fine tower.

The Florentine artist stayed five years—from 1540 to 1545—which was quite a record for a man of his combative nature. So was the fact that during his stay he never had anything but praise for Francis his master.

He fought with everyone else. Most of the trouble was over gold—gold to use in his actual work and more gold in payment for what he made. Two of his early creations for Francis were a beautiful vase and basin. Francis asked him for a saltcellar to go with them, and Cellini produced a wax model which he had brought along from Italy.

"This is a hundred times finer than I had dreamed," Francis said. "You are truly an astounding man. You never seem to rest, and you should never be allowed to!" He ordered his Treasurer to supply a thousand crowns' worth of "old gold of good weight" for the new project.

The Treasurer, a certain Vicomte d'Orbec, kept Cellini waiting until late at night. Finally, with the gold stowed in a wicker basket, the artist started back along the Seine to his home and workshop. He was wearing a good coat of mail and carried short sword and dagger.

About five hundred paces from the château de Nesle, Cellini was jumped in the dark by four footpads.

"If you want my sword and my cape," he cried, "you won't have them without getting hurt."

He attacked vigorously, thinking it safer than retreating. At the same time, as he cut and parried, he yelled for help. At last, some of his own people heard his cries and came running. Four servants with pikes quickly routed the robbers.

"Those four cowards couldn't even take a thousand gold crowns from a man weighed down by the gold," Cellini exulted.

"You have too much confidence in yourself," his chief steward reproached him. "One of these days you will cause us real grief."

Cellini never was able to prove that d'Orbec was the man behind the attack. But he makes it clear in the diary that he himself was convinced of it.

Later, Cellini carved a new entrance for the palace of

Fontainebleau. Over the door was a wonderful reclining nymph, with many roe deer, stags, and greyhounds. It was a masterpiece as fine as his great *Perseus with the Head of Medusa,* which is still in the Loggia dei Lanzi in his native Florence.

During Cellini's time, Francis was greatly troubled over the never-ending rivalry with Charles V and the prospect of renewed hostilities. One day, to cheer him up, the sculptor uncovered the model of a fountain with a heroic figure of Mars in the middle and smaller statues at the corners. The corner statues, he explained, represented Letters, Music, the Graphic Arts, and fourthly, "the Liberality without which the others would not be possible."

As he tells it, Cellini saved his best line for last: "Your Majesty is Mars, for in you there is all courage, and you use it wisely for the sacred defense of your glory."

"I have found a man after my own heart," Francis answered. "My friend"—and here he gave Cellini a hearty clap on the back—"I don't know which of the two pleasures is the greater: that of a prince who finds a man after his own heart or that of an artist of talent who finds a prince to give him all the means to express his brilliant inspirations."

"If I am the person you are talking about," Cellini with uncharacteristic modesty answered, "my good fortune is without doubt greater by far."

"Let's agree then that our luck is equal," said the King with a laugh.

The fact was that this mutual-admiration society worked very well, with splendid results. It is sad that so much of

Gold saltceller by Cellini

Cellini's magic work has been melted down, but the nymph is in the Louvre and the saltcellar, with its tilted figures of Neptune and Cybele in perfect balance, is in the great art museum in Vienna.

While he pleased the King, Cellini, by his truculence and his talent, made many enemies. One was Primaticcio, who was jealous of his skill, and another was Anne de Heilly, Duchesse d'Étampes. By now firmly entrenched as the King's mistress, she was jealous of the time that he and the artist spent together.

Mistress and lesser artist conspired against Cellini. First they caused a lot of ancient Roman statues to be recast in bronze. Theoretically, they were to form a background for the unveiling of a new statue of Cellini's in the loggia at Fontainebleau. The real idea was that their perfection would put Cellini's work to shame.

Cellini's statue was a flamboyant Jupiter hurling thunderbolts with his raised right hand. Alerted about the plot, the sculptor placed a torch among the thunderbolts for greater effect, and put his statue on a movable platform.

Here is the scene of the unveiling, as reconstructed from the Italian's contemporary-seeming diary:

The King arrives at the open area, where the statues are on display. He has dined well, and is relaxed and in the mood to be amused. In his company are the Duchesse d'Étampes . . . his own beloved sister Marguerite and her second husband, the King of Navarre . . . the Dauphin and his wife . . . and several lords who have been briefed by the King's mistress. Their assignment: to talk loudly against Cellini and his "tawdry" new statue, which they do.

The King goes straight toward the Jupiter, which Cellini is moving in his direction on its platform.

"It is the most beautiful work I have ever seen," Francis cries when he nears it. "I love the arts and am versed in them. Nevertheless, I would never have imagined the hundredth part of the pleasure I feel."

"It is perfectly clear that you have no eyes," Anne says boldly. "Don't you see all those beautiful antique statues in the background? That is where the true merit is, not in modern baubles like this."

The courtiers take up the cry, exclaiming over the copies of the classic statues.

The King says dryly that these copies make Cellini's work seem more marvelous than ever. "We must hold Benvenuto in great esteem," he adds. "For his works not only bear comparison with the antique ones, they surpass them."

Anne protests that the Cellini Jupiter is a trick of lighting, and would have far less beauty by day. She even implies that the light scarf around the nude male figure is to conceal certain imperfections in the casting, done to save money.

Cellini, furious, wrenches off the scarf. It is clear that the sculptor has cut no corners. Francis laughs, but Anne resumes the attack.

Cellini defends himself stoutly. "I am not accountable for my works to anyone but His Majesty," he maintains.

"And what would you say if you had to be accountable to others as well?"

"I wouldn't stay here if I had to."

"Suppose it was to me?"

"If I had to do that, I would not stay with His Majesty."

"Enough! Enough!" the King interposes, less amused now. Restless as usual, he prepares to leave the scene. Cellini starts to remonstrate with Anne again.

"Benvenuto, I forbid you to open your mouth. Calm yourself. I will give you more gold than you want."

In a lighter vein, Clément Marot, like Leonardo and Cellini, was a man after Francis's own heart. His was a poetry of smiles, and his occasional verse—in the sense of verse to mark occasions and events—was almost always graceful, neat, and to the point. He was in effect the poet laureate of France, and Francis kept him in his household and enjoyed his cheerful company.

There was something childish about Marot. He had a puckish, harlequin side which kept getting him into trouble. His rhymed translation of the Psalms was all the rage, but some thought the verses lacking in proper religious respect. He flirted with the Protestant ideas that were spreading through France in the 1530's. For this he was placed under mild arrest by the Bishop of Chartres and confined in a comfortable house near the Episcopal Palace there.

To cheer Marot up, the people of Chartres came and sang his own songs to him under his window. He was soon released, for it was well known that the King was his patron. But finally, as the mood of France darkened and Francis himself grew older and less well, Marot slipped away, ending his days in Protestant Geneva.

Another of the King's protégés, in a much less familiar way, was the incomparable François Rabelais, the "Michelangelo of laughter," the ex-monk whose many-faceted genius almost matched Leonardo's own.

Born at Chinon in 1493, he took Benedictine orders. In 1530 he simply walked out of the monastery. Rabelais wore his monkish cowl all his life, but from then on his life was anything but holy. For some months he wandered about, then set himself up as a physician in Montpellier. In 1532, at Lyons, he performed the first dissection of a corpse before students ever attempted in France. His great gusty book, *Pantagruel,* came out in 1533, and it was followed two years later by *Gargantua.* Rabelais mocked everything from celibacy to astrology to monarchy. Theologians and pompous scholars were especial targets of his tumultuous prose. Pantagruel, although his story came first, is the son of the giant Gargantua. Born with a thirst, educated in a manner not unlike Francis I's own, he is the Renaissance prince of princes, larger than life and far more amusing.

Rabelais's satire came pretty close to the throne. On the subject of fools that he had suffered, he said that there was "the metaphysical fool, the predestined fool, the fool elect, and the fool imperial." He believed in freedom in all things: over the portal of his imaginary Abbey of Thélème are the words, *Faye ce que vouldras,* meaning simply "Do what you please."

For his attacks on the Sorbonne, the establishment, and the monasteries, he was always in or near trouble. Once Francis summoned him to the Court, and many thought his great star had run its course. But Rabelais emerged smiling from his talk with the King, and it was quickly known that Francis had congratulated him on his books.

On September 17, 1545, Francis gave Rabelais his permission to print the third volume of the series, containing the further adventures of Pantagruel, King of Utopia, and his friend Panurge.

After the death of his royal protector, Rabelais thought it wise to move to Rome for a while. He died in 1553, his style remaining pungently Rabelaisian to the end. As he lay dying he said, "Let down the curtain, the farce is over."

His last words were "I go to seek the great perhaps."

Chapter 25

A SADDENING
OF YEARS

By the summer of 1531, Louise of Savoy was dying and she knew it. She was only fifty-five, but her body was ravaged by disease and she was crippled by gout. She was at Fontaine-bleau in August but wished to see her own beloved Romo-rantin once more. With Marguerite of Angoulême in faith-ful attendance, she journeyed as far south as Grez-en-Gâtinais. She could go no farther and there, on September 22, she breathed her last.

Francis was at Chantilly when he heard the news. Hating to be in the presence of sickness and death, he had failed to come to her bedside, nor did he attend Louise's magnificent state funeral in October. What he did do was write her epitaph, and it leaves no doubt what his true feelings for his mother were:

> Here lies the body, whose soul, become glorious,
> Lies in His arms, Who holds her precious.
> What say you France, in what terms of honor
> Do you voice your lament of her, the great donor?

Through sixteen more lines his torment shows clearly. Louise had indeed been the great donor, for she had given her life to France and her son. To France she had twice brought her steady hand as regent, and a real measure of peace at the last. To Francis, she gave a devotion not unmixed with the love of power, but which had never wavered—even when, as in her dying days, he failed her badly.

The celebrated trinity was breaking up. Marguerite had married, in 1527, the cool and rather slippery Henry d'Albret, King of Navarre. So she was away a good deal at Pau and Nérac, the two main towns of that small state in the Pyrenees. The marriage was no love match but a political measure at Francis's wish. He needed Navarre, which sat in its strategic mountain saddle between France and Spain, and he needed d'Albret, who was nimble and tended to play his two great neighbors off against each other.

Henry was six years younger than his famous bride. They had one daughter, Jeanne d'Albret, Queen of Navarre in her own good time. She in turn was the mother of Henry of Navarre, who became the great Henry IV of France.

The 1530's were a period of rapid change. The old faces were fast disappearing from the European scene. Clement VII died in 1534, worn out by his lifelong efforts to please all comers. Shortly before his death he had agreed to the marriage of his niece, Catherine de' Medici, to Francis's second son, Henry, Duke of Orléans. This seemed a splendid idea at the time, especially since it annoyed Charles V very much indeed. Later, the infiltration of Medici blood into the royal line would have near-disastrous results for France.

Cardinal Wolsey, a stout friend of France, had died in 1530, and five years later France's own great political prince of the Church, Cardinal Duprat, also passed on, while still Chancellor. No longer young, and with all his best adventures far behind him, Fleuranges the Young Adventurer died in 1537, exhausted by his wounds and his wars. (He had been made a Marshal of France during his captivity; he never did resume the diary.)

The new top men were the hard-bitten, driving Duke of Montmorency, who became Constable of France in 1538, and Chabot de Brion, the High Admiral in succession to Bonnivet. Like his predecessor, de Brion was a cheerful, well-liked man. He had shared Francis's imprisonment, and gained the King's friendship during those trying months.

France was prospering. Her fine cities—Paris, Lyons, Tours, and Rouen in particular—grew and throve. Her wheat and wine, her cloths and silks, were sought in all the markets of Europe. A little late in the day, her hardy mariners, including Giovanni da Verrazano and Jacques Cartier, began with royal encouragement to probe the New World.

Despite France's prosperity and vigor, the skies were darkening. Charles V, the implacable enemy, was lining up new allies such as Savoy on her eastern borders. There was no question but that Charles considered a resurgent France a direct menace to his Empire.

Worse still, the Protestant movement was casting its somber shadow across France and undermining the health of the whole body politic.

The French word for Protestant was Huguenot. It prob-
ably derives from the Flemish words *Huis Genooten* or
"house fellows." These were students who gathered in each
other's rooms to study the Bible. In the 1520's a new translation of the Scriptures began to circulate in France. It was
written by one Jacques Lefèvre, and it had a great and growing impact. The Huguenots based their dissent in good part
on this book, and on their right to their own individual in-
terpretation of its contents.

These early Huguenots were artisans, small businessmen
and the like, people who lived mostly in the cities and towns.
Only one percent came from the nobility, and another one
percent were clergymen who were at odds with the established Church.

By the end of the 1540's, there were some 750,000 Huguenots in France, meeting in over 2,000 assemblies and im-
promptu churches. Their reforming spirit was not just di-
rected against rigid Catholic doctrine, which had not
permitted any new interpretations of Holy Writ for many
centuries. Thriving members of the bourgeois class, they reflected the bold new spirit of the Renaissance as well.

They received a good deal of their inspiration from a brilliant Frenchman called John Calvin. Calvin's creed was a
stern one. Dancing and card playing were forbidden, even
on weekdays. He thundered against statues in churches,
crucifixes, altar decorations—all the rich symbolism of Chris-
tianity. The heart and core of the doctrine was something
called Predestination. In essence, it maintained that man had
some control over his own destiny: by righteous living he
might earn eternal life. This suited these independent-

minded middle-class citizens very well. *Work hard, live a clean life, and you may be saved!*

At first Francis was tolerant. By that Concordat of 1516 he controlled the high Church offices. Church revenues in large degree stayed in France. He had no quarrel with Rome, no real incentive to help reform Mother Church. For a while the Reformers did not seem to be a major political hazard. Besides, he himself was something less than a fanatic Catholic. We have seen that his *foi de gentilhomme* was in a way his true faith. He was inclined to let matters jog along, hoping that the Huguenots would not create any irreparable schism or split.

Marguerite went even farther. Intellectually, she was fascinated by the new doctrines. She corresponded with Calvin and was on good terms with the other Huguenot leaders.

The Huguenots were their own worst enemies. Some of the more fanatic took to destroying statues. They would post lookouts in the streets in the dead of night, slip into the churches, hammer in hand, and swing into action. Such were the *iconoclasts,* the destroyers of images, and they did themselves great harm.

The first desecration of this kind took place in Paris in 1528. On May 31 of that year, during the feast of the Pentecost, a statue of the Virgin near the Porte Saint-Antoine was found headless and mutilated. A thrill of horror shivered through France, for the cult of the Virgin was among the most fervent of all. Francis's own strong sense of order and the fitness of things was shocked: he offered a thousand crowns for the capture of the culprit, and ordered a new silver statue to replace the mutilated one.

The real reactionaries, in the prosecutions that soon began, were the Parlement and the Sorbonne. Francis did his best to protect some of the less violent reformers. Twice he intervened to save Louis de Berquin, a high-minded scholar who had translated Martin Luther into French. But in April 1529, Francis was away in Touraine. In his absence, the Parlement, with full support from the Sorbonne, quickly brought Berquin to trial again, condemned him, and burned him alive for heresy.

For five years, the forces of reaction lay low. They had defied the King and gotten away with it. Francis, still not believing that the Reform movement was a tearing danger to the fabric of France, did his best to calm the situation, and succeeded quite well.

Then, in 1534 came the Affair of the Placards. During the night of October 17, big, blasphemous anti-Catholic posters blossomed all over Paris, Orléans, Tours, and Amboise. Full of abuse against the Pope and his "vermin of Cardinals," against the intent and spirit of the Mass, these placards were the work of fanatics who had lost all control.

One of the posters was nailed on the door of the royal chambers at Amboise, where Francis was staying at the time. Here was rude evidence of real conspiracy. It was obvious that even members of the King's household were involved. Alarmed at last, Francis put out an edict which decreed death by burning for those who preached heresy or shouted it too loudly.

This was all that Parlement and the Sorbonne needed to go into action. They fought terror with terror, and the terrible glow of martyrs at the stake lit up the land. The actual number of deaths was not more than several score, but they took place all over France. The tolerant Francis had come down on the side of law and order at last, and these persecutions would continue in varying intensity for the rest of his reign.

In 1536 John Calvin fled to Switzerland. There he soon published his most famous work, *Institutes of the Christian Religion,* with an eloquent preface addressed to the "very magnificent, very magnanimous" Francis I. From Geneva, where he finally settled, Calvin continued to be the spiritual leader of the Huguenots and to loose his thunderbolts, until his death eighteen years later. 1554

As a counter-measure to the Reform movement, the new Pope, Paul III, moved vigorously to put the established Church in order. Its disciplined vanguard—the shock troops of the Catholic campaign—were the members of the Order of the Society of Jesus, founded by Saint Ignatius Loyola in 1534. The Jesuits, as they came to be called, proved just as zealous in the Lord's work as Calvin's own austere legions.

In 1536 Charles V invaded Provence with a splendid army of 47,000 men. But his attempt to lead men in battle was a total fiasco. Charged by Francis to defend this southeast corner of his kingdom, Montmorency reduced it to a desert. He poisoned the wells, ruined the crops, left the villages open and empty. Only three towns were defended—but they were so strongly manned that Charles could not take them.

"The Emperor claims that Provence is land that belongs to him," said the duke. "We must turn it over to him so that he can bury his men in it."

After two months Charles had had enough. He turned tail without ever fighting a pitched battle, leaving two-thirds of his army behind as victims of the scorched-earth policy and the guerrilla tactics of the hard-driving duke. It was a far cry from Melegnano—Pavia, even—and the age of chivalry.

That same year, Francis suffered a terrible family tragedy. His son and namesake the Dauphin, eighteen years old and the star of his three sons, died under circumstances that pointed to poison. After a game of tennis, he gulped a goblet of cold water. Shortly afterward he was in agony, and three days later he was dead.

His squire, an Italian called Montecuculi, had given him the fatal cup. Under torture he confessed, then disavowed his confession. He was condemned to be drawn and quartered by four wild horses. The dread sentence was quickly carried out, but it did not give Francis back his beloved son.

Henry, Duke of Orléans at the time, became heir apparent. A melancholy boy of sixteen, he had suffered far more from the Spanish imprisonment than his resilient brother. The four years in isolation had done something to his somber soul. Smoldering hatred of all things Spanish was one result. An almost childlike dependence on Diane de Poitiers, the cool, fascinating Duchesse de Valentinois, was another. Almost twenty-two years his senior, she was mother and mistress to Henry all his grown life. He only tolerated his own wife Catherine de' Medici because Diane told him to.

In 1537 another death shook Francis. His frail and favorite daughter Madeleine, married a few months before to King James of Scotland, failed to survive the damp and cold of her first Scottish year.

So, with family tragedy and religious strife at home, and war clouds ever present along the frontiers, Francis and France saddened into the 1540's.

Chapter 26

THE ENDLESS RIVALRY

One episode in the last year of the 1530's showed Francis at his most magnanimous. This was the state visit of Charles V to France.

The city of Ghent in the Low Countries was, it seemed, in open revolt. The Emperor wished to take action against it in person, as an object lesson to other restless cities of his polyglot domains. Could he save time and a dangerous sea journey by traveling through his dear brother-in-law's realm?

On one of those generous impulses of the kind that Charles himself would never have, Francis agreed to the visit. When he informed his Council of the decision, several members urged him to attach some conditions.

"No," said the King, "when you do a generous thing, you must do it completely and boldly."

Later that same day, the King came upon the Court fool, Triboulet, who was busily writing something in his Fool's Diary. It turned out to be the name of the Emperor. Francis asked why.

"A bigger fool than I," he explained to his master, "if he comes passing through France."

"What will thou say if I let him pass?" asked the King.

"I will rub out his name and put in yours in its place."

Charles had a bad cold when he arrived at Bayonne. He snuffled all the way to Châtellerault, where the King greeted him. From Poitou to Paris there were hunts and pigeon shoots, banquets, masks and balls, in honor of the Imperial guest and his train.

At Amboise the Emperor's recurring gout was so bad that he had to ride his carriage up the spiral roadway inside the great tower. Francis turned the arrival into a splendid ceremony. Horsemen with flaming torches were massed on the drawbridge, and the ramp itself was lined with foot soldiers with more torches, making the night into day.

At Blois, Chambord, Orléans, and Fontainebleau, Francis dazzled him with the wealth and industry of his country.

"There is not in the world any greatness such as that of a King of France," said Charles, impressed but not entirely happy.

Charles and his host reached Paris on January 1, 1540, and spent a week there. During this time, Francis was under heavy pressure to take the Emperor prisoner and exact many concessions and hard conditions for his release. To his eternal credit, he resisted the temptation.

There were two awkward moments.

One day the King's reckless third son jumped on the crupper of the Emperor's horse. Throwing his arms around him, the boy shouted, "Your Imperial Majesty is my prisoner!" Charles didn't even turn his head. He put his horse to the full gallop while the young prince clung on for dear life.

On another occasion, Francis and Anne de Heilly were chatting with the Emperor.

"Brother," said the King, "here is a fair lady who thinks I

should not let you out of Paris until you revoke the Treaty of Madrid."

"If the advice is sound," said Charles icily, "follow it."

From then on, the visitor made a special effort to cultivate the duchess. At one point she was holding a basin for him to rinse his Imperial hands. Charles very neatly plopped a big diamond ring into the basin—and she became less urgent about his being made prisoner.

On the way north from Paris, Charles was splendidly entertained by the Duke of Montmorency at his castle of Chantilly. It was here that the Emperor made a promise that showed how nervous he was on French soil.

Montmorency was urging him to recognize France's never-abandoned claims to the duchy of Milan.

"No," said Charles, "I must not bind myself as long as I am in your power. When I have chastised my rebellious subjects, I will content your King."

Later, when he was out of France and the rebellion of Ghent had been brutally suppressed, Charles spoke quite differently: "Let not the King of France if he be wise put himself at my mercy as I have been at his, for I swear by the living God that he would not be free until he gave up Burgundy, and Champagne as well."

The fact was that Charles was furiously jealous of Francis, of his easy charm, his prosperous kingdom, and comparatively loyal subjects. So the state visit, for all its surface good will, turned sour. The endless rivalry began all over again— only Charles was now the angry aggressor. Francis's chivalry was back in place, his faith in himself as gentleman reconfirmed.

The same old jockeying for allies set in, more cynically

than ever. In 1543 Charles V and Henry VIII formed a new coalition against France, and Francis shocked Christian Europe by signing a treaty calling for joint military action with Suleiman the Turk.

When the Venetian ambassador to Paris complained about the working agreement with the Sultan, Francis's reply shows how bitter the rivalry with Charles had grown. "Sir ambassador," said the King, "I cannot deny that I eagerly desire to see the Turk very powerful and ready for war; not on his own account, for he is an infidel and all we are Christians, but in order to cripple the power of the Emperor, to force him into great expense, and to give all other governments security against so great an enemy."

Charles not only denied having made any promises while Francis's guest, he also allowed two French ambassadors to be murdered while crossing his German lands.

Francis, the injured party, declared war—a war that was in any event inevitable.

By April 1544, the main French army and the Spanish one were concentrated around the little Piedmontese town of Ceresole on the Italian side of the Alps. The forces were evenly matched, with about 20,000 men each. But the young and dashing French commander, the Comte d'Enghien, was under royal orders not to attack. Having learned the lesson of Pavia, his aging King did not want to risk all in a single engagement.

D'Enghien sent a fighting cock called Blaise de Monluc to try to convince Francis to let him give battle. The King was at Fontainebleau, where his diminishing energies were very much taken up with the creation of the beautiful long gallery which bears his name.

Monluc was a wiry Gascon with a gift of words. The King and his Council listened closely to his arguments (the King had dined well and was a little indolent and sleepy at first). But they also seemed to have one ear attuned to the voice of caution.

Monluc's main theme was boldness.

"We are in great heart, and they are in fear," he said. In his climactic words, he spoke directly to his warrior King: "It is not greatness of numbers that wins, but a sound heart. In the name of God, Sire, have no fear in granting our wish. Let me not return with the shame of saying that you fear to place the chances of battle in our hands—we who freely and boldly offer you our lives."

Francis hesitated, conferred a long time with his advisors. But he had recognized in Monluc the irresistible spirit of Melegnano and his own youth.

He rose at last, and the years, the heavy flesh, and lack-luster eye, were gone for the moment.

"Let them fight! Let them fight!" he shouted.

Ceresole was a stunning victory for the French. Artillery, musketry, and a well-timed cavalry charge of great verve all contributed. The Imperial forces left 8,000 men on the field of battle. French losses were 200! Among the enormous quantity of loot was a jewel-encrusted watch belonging to the Spanish commander, the Marquis du Guast. The Duchesse de Nevers, sister of the victorious d'Enghien, presented it to Francis in due time.

"Sire," she said, "we can't present the Marquis du Guast to you right at the moment. He escaped at great speed on a fine Spanish horse; but here is his watch, which apparently was not as well mounted."

Such was the last real flare-up of the King's old fighting spirit. The truth was that he had lost interest in war, now that he no longer could take part himself, now that he saw clearly that all it ever did was lead to more war.

So, a little easily, a little hastily perhaps, considering the splendid feat of arms of Ceresole, he made peace. But there were good reasons to do so. Henry VIII, in character, was nibbling away at Boulogne, and Charles himself had made a tentative pass at Paris from the east.

The Treaty of Crespy, signed in September of 1544, left everything about as it had been. But at least Francis was now free to turn, more fully than ever, to the area of his lasting fame.

Chapter 27

T I M E   O F   S O L S T I C E

He stayed at Fontainebleau as much as his increasing restlessness allowed him to stay anywhere. The long gallery there
was nearly done, with its use of fresco, stucco, and wood in
sensuous harmony unlike anything seen before. Already, he
was planning the ballroom which would, when finished,
bear his son Henry's initials entwined forever with Diane's.

His efforts to invigorate the French language were paying
off. Back in 1536, the decree which he issued at Villers-
Cotterêts had ordered all official business to be done in
French rather than Latin. This had been the great first incentive. Now poets, writers, scientists, theologians were finding French the suppler, more natural tongue.

Francis knew well that writing, however brilliant, was not
enough. To be read, writers had to be published, and in read-
able form. So he gave his high-placed enthusiasm to support
the master printers of the day, the Estienne brothers and
Claude Garamond among them. We have a glimpse of
Francis riding over to Robert Estienne's workshop in the
rue Saint-Jean de Beauvais to pay a surprise call—and wait-

ing cheerfully in the anteroom while the master finished reading some proofs.

Royally sponsored and befriended, Claude Garamond created new roman and italic type faces that marked a sharp break with the cumbersome old Gothic lettering.

The King also kept a trained eye on his palaces, where construction was forever going on. At Blois there was the high, arcaded wing. In his unmistakable way Henry James has described it: "This exquisite, this extravagant, this transcendent piece of architecture is the most joyous utterance of the French Renaissance." And there was the wondrous outdoor staircase, counterpart to the enclosed one at Chambord.

The Louvre was the most French of his reconstructions, for he picked new native talent for his purposes there—Pierre Lescot the architect and Jean Goujon the sculptor.

He liked to visit the fine seaport of Le Havre de Grâce, which he himself had begun in 1515. Fortifications and new deepwater jetties were making it into the most modern of sea citadels. He resisted pressure from his courtiers to call it Francisopolis, and in time it became just Le Havre, for the haven it was.

With Francis's hand at the helm, his fleet grew from 30 galleys in 1536 to 210 by the middle 1540's. The flagship, the sumptuous *Grande Françoise,* though never very seaworthy, was one of the wonders of the time.

He corresponded with Erasmus, the famous scholar, and he wrote Michelangelo to bid for a masterpiece or two, "for I have great need for a sample of your work."

The royal collection, at the Louvre and elsewhere, was

Circular staircase at Blois

the largest in Europe. Consisting of over 500 pictures, it showed his catholic taste, for there were Flemish and French canvases as well as Italian. Bosch, Breughel, and Clouet were linked with such masters as Titian, Michelangelo, Raphael, and Leonardo.

The Collège de France, founded by Francis in 1529 "for research and the advancement of science," grew in fame as a kind of antidote to the entrenched, reactionary Sorbonne. It was a college of people, not stone and mortar—a series of lectures fostered by Francis and giving him great satisfaction.

If he no longer lived in fire like his emblem the salamander, he had done his best to extinguish it, as the second half of his motto proclaimed.

So now, in the peaceful marriage of French and Italian taste which formed the High Renaissance, he was the royal matchmaker. Who is to say which is the more beautiful? Something about the final blend—the exuberant, sometimes overpowering Italian architecture and the subtler, more joyous French, with its softer lines—was incomparable.

It is perhaps no accident that the word for the age is the French *Renaissance* rather than the Italian *Risorgimento,* despite the fact that France was a latecomer in the many new forms of art.

Francis's role has been described by an unknown chronicler of the seventeenth century in words that sum it up as well as any. "He had," wrote the chronicler, "a noble passion for all things beautiful."

In his last years he indulged this passion to the full. It was to occupy more and more of his time and his diminishing vitality.

He was also busy with the sad business of getting ready to die.

Chapter 28

DEATH OF A
GENTLEMAN OF FRANCE

The magnificent machine that was Francis was slowing down. His body was racked by recurring fever, his voice was a hoarse whisper now. He was subject to spells of brooding melancholy.

There has been a good deal of speculation about exactly what the disease was which pulled him down. His detractors say syphilis, but this diagnosis was not made until 1603, over fifty years after his death. Cancer of the throat—unknown in his day—seems more likely.

We have a description of the King, written early in 1547, which goes a long way toward refuting the syphilis theory. Mario Cavalli, the Venetian ambassador, put down his observations in a report at the end of his French tour of duty. The comments on the King are as accurate and impartial as any, for he had no axe to grind:

The King is now in his fifty-fourth year; his aspect is entirely royal, so that if one had never seen his face or his portrait, on first seeing him one would at once say: that is the King! His every movement is so noble and majestic

*that there is no prince like him. His temperament is robust,
in spite of the excesses of fatigue to which he has always
been subject and to which he is still subject on his many
expeditions and journeys.*

Cavalli goes on to give an estimate of the King's character
in these autumnal years.

*In regard to great affairs of state, and to war and peace,
His Majesty, conciliatory in all else, wishes others to obey
his will. In these instances there is no one at the Court,
of however great authority, who dares remonstrate with
His Majesty . . . He pardons faults readily, even as he
reconciles himself gladly with those he has offended; he
is also by temperament always ready to give, although the
necessities of the times have somewhat tempered his generous impulses.*

Francis knew he was going down, but he also knew how
to go down like a king.

He saw the gleam in his son Henry's eye—the gleam that
said *some day all this will be mine*—and it saddened him.
He remembered how he himself had watched Louis XII the
way Henry and the rest of them watched him now.

The Duke of Montmorency had become completely
Henry's man and the Dauphin called him "my father."
Diane de Poitiers had of course linked her destiny for a long
time to Francis's son's—and so, more recently, had the near-
royal family of Guise. They were all waiting in the wings

Francis I on horseback, late sixteenth-century French painting

for the old war horse to answer the last call of the trumpet.

Out of his melancholy and his boredom came that terrible restlessness. He could never be anywhere for more than a week or two, even in his "delicious deserts of Fontainebleau," where he could be alone with his pictures and his books. So the Court was a vagabond one, moving endlessly to every province of France.

A French proverb says "to say goodbye is to die a little." In his own way the dying Francis was saying goodbye to his fair land.

The ritual of these royal visits did not vary much. The city or town would be warned well in advance so that the richer citizens could hang out tapestries in welcome. Triumphal arches were set up in the outskirts and the poor people given decorated sheets to wave as he passed.

At the city gate the mayor and principal officials waited with the keys of the city on a cushion. The King would look at the keys and then invariably return them with one of those royal gestures he made so well.

In the main square, scenes from his life or from mythology would be staged for his pleasure. The killing of the wild boar at Amboise was a favorite theme, the knighthood bestowed by Bayard on the field of Melegnano another.

There would be a banquet at the castle that night, and days of hunting, jousting, and water sports would follow. But first of all, before the state dinner, Francis would put on the great closed crown of France, topped by its *fleur de lis* of solid gold, and receive the oath of fealty from his loyal subjects.

After a week or so, the royal cavalcade, often several

thousand strong, would pass again under the triumphal arches. By now the arches tended to look a little worn and faded, and so were the good people of the city or town. Mingled with their pride that Francis had come was the very French awareness of the cost, and the hope that he would stay away a long, long time.

In January of 1547, Francis had news which shocked him more than he had expected: Henry VIII of England was dead. They had not met for fifteen years and had never really been friends. But they had been young together, and glorious. Francis brooded.

His answer was always to go somewhere. In January and February, the itinerant Court visited nine places, beginning with Compiègne and ending with Rochefort. At the end of February, he came to the castle of Rambouillet, west of Paris on the Chartres road.

It was an agreeable little castle, brick-walled, with three pepper-pot towers and a surrounding moat. It belonged to Francis's captain of the guard, Jacques d'Angennes, and the King planned to stay just one night there. But the hunting in the nearby forest was good and he stayed longer. Then his fever came back and he took to his bed. Purges, a rigid diet, bleedings exacted their toll of his strength. Soon it was clear that he would never leave the bed again.

The Dauphin was summoned. Henry was twenty-eight now, a handsome man with his father's powerful build but no spark to relieve his somber spirit. He stood dutifully by the bedside while Francis spoke to him in his hoarse whisper: "Above all I commend to you this kingdom, whose people are the best and most obedient, whose nobility is the most faithful and devoted to their King that could be. I have found them such and so you will find them. So, love your kingdom and its riches better than yourself, and better than any of the things of earth, after the love of God."

These may or may not have been his exact words, but they sound in character. They become him. He went on to warn Henry against women who dominate, thinking more about Diane de Poitiers than about his own Anne de Heilly, who was sobbing her heart out in the next room.

He also warned Henry against the ambition of the house of Guise. Noticing how glum his son looked, Francis even tried to cheer him up a little.

"I have lived my part," he said as his voice grew fainter still. "Now that I know that I am leaving as my successor a prince as wise as you are, I die the happiest man in the world . . ."

He heard mass. He kissed the Cross and held it for a long time in his arms. Just at the end, long after he seemed to have lost both sight and speech, he whispered the name of Jesus.

Thus died Francis, the first of his name, on the last day of March in the year 1547.

Louis XII's *gros garçon* had not spoiled everything, as his father-in-law had so sourly predicted he would do. He left

France far more powerful than he found her. He gave her what she wanted: strong central authority and pride in herself as a nation.

To find his truest epitaph we have to go back to that sunburned land of the Charente, with its white roads and gently rolling vineyards. The town of Cognac there seems half forgotten now, despite the fact that its business of distilling brandy has made its name a household word. The castle on the slow-moving river is not much as French castles go—a range of simple stone buildings, some fine vaulted rooms, a tower or two.

But under the one good bay window on the river side there is a modest plaque. On the plaque is an inscription, which reads like this:

IN THIS CASTLE OF THE VALOIS

WAS BORN

ON THE TWELFTH OF SEPTEMBER 1494

FRANCIS THE FIRST

KING OF FRANCE (1515–1547)

PROTECTOR OF THE ARTS, OF SCIENCE,

AND OF LETTERS

He himself would have taken pride in the inscription. For those last two lines contain the essence of his enduring glory.

Epilogue

Marguerite of Angoulême was at one of her favorite retreats, the Convent of Tusson not far from Cognac, in late March of 1547. One night there she had a terrible dream. In it, her brother—pale as death—was calling to her from afar. "My sister, my sister!" he cried. Then his voice seemed to falter, and she woke in terror.

It was the exact moment of Francis's death. She had known he was ill, and had sent a messenger to Rambouillet to bring back news. When he returned, the good nuns concealed the sad tidings from her. Then one day, two weeks after the King's death, she heard someone sobbing. It was a poor mad nun who blurted out the truth when Marguerite asked why she was crying.

Marguerite lived two more years. But her heart was broken, her life had lost its meaning. She poured out her grief in verse, and death when it came was almost welcome. Only just at the end did this much-loved princess find that she was reluctant to die—even to join the brother whom she had loved more than life.

As for the Emperor Charles, he went into retirement in

1555, more like a merchant than a monarch. First he divided his vast lands. The Empire—mostly German and Austrian lands—went to his younger brother Ferdinand. The Lowlands, Spain, the Italian holdings, and the New World he gave to his son Philip II.

It was an admission of a failure. Francis and France had won. The crushing jaws never closed and now the fulcrum was broken; there was no real leverage any more.

Henry II sent one more expedition into Italy. It was led by the ambitious Francis of Guise, and it was a miserable fiasco.

Both Henry and Ferdinand, the new Holy Roman Emperor, were obsessed with stamping out heresy at home. So was Philip of Spain, under whom the dread Inquisition reached fever pitch. So they all made peace—at Cateau-Cambrésis in 1559.

The next thirty years were one of the darkest times in French history. Even though external perils were mostly over, religious-political war raged internally and compulsively.

Henry II died from a jousting accident in the same year that the Treaty of Cateau-Cambrésis was signed. His three sons ruled in turn. But the infusion of Medici blood through Catherine, their mother, had brought strange results. The Valois line became a tainted and dying one. At best Francis II, Charles IX, and Henry III were weak and indolent. At worst they were cruel and demented, as Charles IX in particular was. His massacre of the Huguenots on the night of Saint Bartholomew was the darkest blot of this dark time. 1572

France survived. Francis's great-nephew, Henry of Navarre, "all French" like his great-uncle, brave and vigorous like him too, became King of France in 1589. This famous grandson of Marguerite of Angoulême brought sanity back to France.

The great brimming river of French history had gone through thirty years of pollution. Now, running in sunlit country again, it purged and cleared itself.

And France, under Henry IV, achieved another time of greatness like good King Francis's golden time.

Chronology

1488—Charles of Angoulême marries Louise of Savoy.

1492—Birth of their first child, Marguerite of Angoulême.

1494—September, King Charles VIII of France invades Italy.

—September 12, birth of Francis of Angoulême, the future Francis I of France.

1498—April 7, death of Charles VIII and succession of Louis XII.

1499—Francis created Duke of Valois.

—Louis XII marries Anne of Brittany.

1506—Meeting of the Estates General at Tours.

1507—Francis goes to the royal Court as heir apparent.

1512—Francis fights his first campaign, in southern France.

1514—Death of Anne of Brittany.

—May 14, Francis marries Claude de France, daughter of Louis XII.

—October 9, Louis XII marries Mary Tudor.

1515—January 1, Louis XII dies and Francis succeeds to the throne.

—August, Francis crosses the Alps and invades Italy.

—September 13–14, the French victory at Melegnano.

1516—The Concordat of Bologna negotiated and signed.

1519—May 3, death of Leonardo da Vinci at Amboise.

—June 28, Charles V, King of Spain and Archduke of Austria, elected Holy Roman Emperor.

1520—June 7, Francis I and Henry VIII meet on the Field of the Cloth of Gold.

1523—The Duke of Bourbon's conspiracy and escape.

1524—Construction of Chambord begins.

—April 30, the death of Bayard, the *chevalier sans peur et sans reproche*.

—October, Francis invades Italy again.

1525—February 25, battle of Pavia.

1525–26—Imprisonment of Francis at Pizzighettone and Madrid.

1526—August, signing of the Treaty of Madrid (January 14) and release of Francis (March 17).

1527—March 6, death of the Duke of Bourbon on the walls of Rome.

—December, the Parlement of Paris meets and repudiates the Treaty of Madrid.

1527—Trial and execution of Jacques de Semblançay.

1529—The Ladies' Peace of Cambrai.

1531—September 22, death of Louise of Savoy.

1534—October 17, the Affair of the Placards.

1536—Death of the Dauphin.

1539—December, state visit of Charles V.

1540–45—Benvenuto Cellini's stay at the French Court.

1544—Battle of Ceresole.

—Peace of Crespy.

1547—March 31, Francis I dies at Rambouillet.

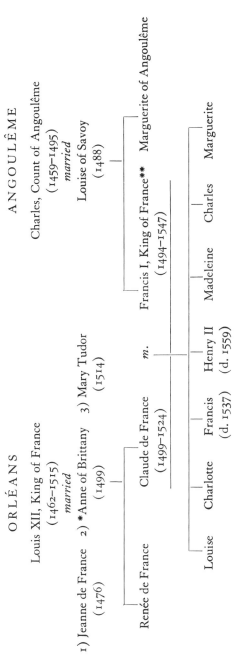

THE ORLÉANS AND ANGOULÊME BRANCHES
OF THE HOUSE OF VALOIS

ORLÉANS

ANGOULÊME

Louis XII, King of France
(1462–1515)
married
1) Jeanne de France   2) *Anne of Brittany   3) Mary Tudor
(1476)   (1499)   (1514)

Charles, Count of Angoulême
(1459–1495)
married
Louise of Savoy
(1488)

Renée de France   Claude de France   *m.*   Francis I, King of France**   Marguerite of Angoulême
                     (1499–1524)   (1494–1547)

Louise   Charlotte   Francis   Henry II   Madeleine   Charles   Marguerite
                       (d. 1537)   (d. 1559)

* Widow of Charles VIII, King of France.
** Francis later married Eleanor of Spain (1530).

Bibliography

IN FRENCH

Bailly, Auguste. *François Ier, Restaurateur des Lettres et des Arts.* Paris: Librairie Arthème Fayard, 1954.

De La Marcke, Robert. *Mémoires du Maréchal Fleuranges.* 2 vols. Paris: Librairie Renouard, 1853. Reissued 1913, 1924.

Dimier, Louis. *Le Château de Fontainebleau et La Cour de François Ier.* Paris: Calmain–Lévy Éditeurs, 1930.

François Ier. Génies et Réalités. Paris: Librairie Hachette, 1967. Contributors include the Duc de Lévis Mirepoix, Philippe Erlanger, Jacques Levron, and Georges Poisson.

Gascar, Pierre. *Chambord.* Paris: Delpire Editeur, 1962.

Gaxotte, Pierre. *Histoire des Français.* 2 vols. Paris, 1951.

Giono, Jean. *Le Désastre de Pavie.* Paris: Gallimard, 1963.

Hanotaux, Gabriel. *Études Historiques sur le XVIième et le XVIIième Siècle en France.* Paris: Librairie Hachette et Cie., 1886.

Lévis Mirepoix, Antoine, Duc de. *François Ier.* Paris: Les Éditions de France, 1931.

Poisson, Georges. *Promenades aux Châteaux de l'Ile de France.* Paris: Éditions André Balland, 1967.

Robida, A. et Toudouze, G. G. *François Ier, le Roi Chevalier.* Paris: Boivin & Cie, Éditeurs, 1909.

Sainte-Beuve, C. A. *Portraits Littéraires.* Vol. III. 1864. Reissue. Paris: Gallimard, 1951.

Sédillot, René. *Survol de l'Histoire de France.* Paris: Club des Librairies de France (Éditions Arthème Fayard), 1959.

Terrasse, Charles. *François Ier; le Roi et le Règne.* 2 vol. Paris: Éditions Bernard Grasset, 1945, 1948.

Zeller, B., ed. *Histoire de France Racontée par les Contemporains.* 6 vols. Paris: Librairie Hachette, 1889, 1890. On Francis I: selections from Fleuranges, Martin and Guillaume du Bellay, Blaise de Monluc, Pierre Brantôme, and others.

IN ENGLISH

Denieul-Cornier, Anne. *A Time of Glory, the Renaissance in France.* Garden City: Doubleday & Company, 1968.

Epton, Nina. *Love and the French.* New York: World, 1959.

Guizot, François Pierre Guillaume. *A Popular History of France.* 6 vols. Boston: Estes and Lauriat, n.d.

Hackett, Francis. *Francis the First.* Garden City: Doubleday, Doran & Co., 1935 (1968 Greenwood).

———. *Henry VIII.* New York: Horace Liveright, 1929.

Huizinga, J. *The Waning of the Middle Ages.* New York: St. Martin's Press, 1949 (reissue).

Lopez, Robert S. *The Three Ages of the Renaissance.* Charlottesville: University Press of Virginia, 1970.

The Loyal Servitor: History of Bayard, the Good Chevalier sans Peur et sans Reproche. Translated from the French of Loredan Larchey. London: Chapman & Hall, 1883.

Mattingly, Garrett. *Catherine of Aragon.* Boston: Little, Brown and Company, 1941 (1960 Vintage Trade Books, Random House).

———. *Renaissance Diplomacy.* Boston: Houghton Mifflin, 1955.

Mayer, Dorothy Moulton. *The Great Regent, Louise of Savoy.* London: Weidenfeld and Nicolson, 1966.

Roche, O. I. A. *The Days of the Upright.* New York: C. N. Potter, 1965.

Rowe, Vivian. *The Loire.* Washington: Robert B. Luce, 1969.

Schneider, Pierre. *Louvre Dialogues.* Translated from the French by Patricia Southgate. New York: Atheneum, 1971.

Sedgwick, Henry Dwight. *France, A Short History*. Boston: Little, Brown and Company, 1929.

Sichel, Edith. *Women and Men of the French Renaissance*. Philadelphia: J. B. Lippincott Company, 1901.

Taylor, Francis Henry. *The Taste of Angels*. Boston: Atlantic–Little, Brown, 1948.

Vallentin, Antonia. *Leonardo da Vinci*. New York: The Viking Press, 1938.

Wernham, Richard Bruce. *Before the Armada*. London: Jonathan Cape, Ltd., 1966.

A NOTE ON MONEY

In the sixteenth century the French *livre* and the British pound were of about equal value. The *livre* was the forerunner of the franc, which eventually replaced it (in 1795). It was worth about 20 cents.

Another much-used coin in the time of Francis I was the *écu*, whose British equivalent was the crown. It was of gold and was the equivalent of six *livres* or $1.20.

Buying power is hard to reckon. Some experts say that a sixteenth-century *livre* or *écu* would be worth twenty times as much today at the very least.

Index